This copy of

THE WITCH'S
OMEN

by Carolyn Keene

belongs to

Sara Louise

Boatwright

Other Sparrow Books
by Carolyn Keene

Mystery of the Stone Tiger
The Riddle of the Frozen Fountain
The Secret of the Silver Dolphin
Mystery of the Wax Queen
The Secret of the Minstrel's Guitar
The Phantom Surfer
The Secret of the Swiss Chalet
The Haunted Lagoon
Mystery of the Bamboo Bird
The Sierra Gold Mystery
The Secret of Lost Lake
The Winking Ruby Mystery
The Ghost in the Gallery
The Curious Coronation
The Hundred-Year Mystery
The Mountain Peak Mystery

Carolyn Keene

The Witch's Omen

SPARROW
BOOKS

A Sparrow Book
Published by Arrow Books Limited
17-21 Conway Street, London W1P 6JD

An imprint of the Hutchinson Publishing Group

London Melbourne Sydney Auckland
Johannesburg and agencies throughout
the world

First published in Great Britain 1984

Printed and bound in Great Britain by
Anchor Brendon Ltd, Tiptree, Essex

ISBN 0 09 933630 8

CONTENTS

CHAPTER I

The Storm Petrel

THE Dana house was bustling with excitement. Halloween masqueraders were arriving at the door in droves asking for treats. A group of young people who had been invited to a party were dancing in the living room to loud and rhythmic stereo music.

"Isn't it exciting?" Jean whispered to her sister Louise. "Just like we planned it."

She readjusted her clown's hat, while Louise, who was dressed in a beautiful, eighteenth century peasant's outfit, gathered her long, wide skirt around her. Then she went to give apples to some little boys at the door. The children thanked her and disappeared into the night.

Louise closed the door behind them, then turned and looked for two visitors who had slipped past her into the house and had gone into the living room.

"Strange," the girl thought to herself. "They didn't even say hello. I wonder who they are."

One of the masqueraders was dressed as a scarecrow. He was apparently a man of medium height, with broad shoulders and a bulging waistline. The other, who was taller, wore a witch's outfit.

Louise went back to the living room, where the two strangers stood watching the dancers. Suddenly the witch grabbed Jean and began to twirl her around. Louise wondered if the scarecrow would ask her to dance, but he stayed where he was, surveying the crowd. Then a friend of the Danas, who was dressed as a wizard, waved to Louise. She danced off with him, still following Jean and the witch with her eyes.

Jean, who had not recognized her partner, asked, "Who are you?"

"I'm the keeper of the storm petrel," the witch answered in a deep voice.

"The storm petrel," Jean repeated. "Isn't that a sea bird?"

"That's right. He follows the ships and predicts storms. He's one of the sailors' best friends."

Jean laughed. "If you're the keeper of a bird, why are you dressed as a witch?"

Her partner stared at her with piercing eyes and did not answer. Jean felt uncomfortable. There was something decidedly strange about this man. Or was the deep voice only a disguise?

Jean doubted this because the witch had large hands, too large for a woman, and his feet appeared to be rather long, too. Before she had a chance to continue the conversation, a gangly astronaut cut in and took her hand, whirling her away from the stranger. Out of the corner of her eye Jean saw the witch and the scarecrow walk into the hall, then her new partner's chatter distracted her for the rest of the dance.

While one of the girls changed the music, Jean looked for Louise and found her talking to the wizard. She motioned for her sister to come over.

"Louise, there was something weird about the witch I danced with. Did you see him?"

Louise nodded. "He came in with a scarecrow. I didn't recognize either of them, and what's more, they just left without saying a word."

"A mystery," Jean muttered.

"What kind of mystery?"

Jean told Louise about the witch's remark regarding the storm petrel. "Maybe it's only a hunch, but the fact that he made this strange remark and stayed only a few minutes makes me suspicious as to why he and the scarecrow came here. I'm sure they were not friends of ours, and we didn't invite them!"

At this moment the girls' Aunt Harriet, with

whom they lived, walked past them toward the hall. "I smell smoke!" she declared.

The girls looked around. None of the guests had been smoking. Jean and Louise followed their aunt out of the living room, and instantly Jean exclaimed, "Look! Smoke's coming from the hall closet!"

Aunt Harriet yanked the door open. A cloth coat was on fire. Acrid smoke poured from it. Louise grabbed the coat, carried it out the front door, and threw it on the lawn. By this time several of the guests had smelled the smoke and hurried into the hall. Looking out the door, they saw Louise stamping hard on the coat. Gary and John, two of the guests, rushed to help her.

"What happened? Whose coat is this?" John asked.

"It's mine," Louise replied. "But I have no idea how it caught on fire!"

The three managed to put out the flames and went back to the closet, where Jean and Aunt Harriet had already begun to look for clues. Jean picked up a cigarette lighter.

"Apparently this was used to set the coat on fire," she declared. "I wonder whose it is."

"None of our friends'," Louise declared. "Perhaps it belongs to the witch or the scarecrow!"

Jean stared at her. "Those two walked out into the hall when the astronaut cut into our dance!" she said excitedly. "You're right, they could have set the fire!"

"But why would they leave this lighter?" John asked. "It looks like a good one."

Jean shrugged. "Perhaps one of them dropped it because he heard someone coming."

By now all the guests had rushed out to the hall and the front lawn. Because of all the paper decorations, the idea of a fire had frightened them badly, and they began to leave.

"Oh, please don't go," Louise pleaded with them. "We have so much to eat."

But their friends, many of them from the neighbourhood, ignored her. They thanked their hostesses for inviting them and hurried out the front door.

Jean heaved a tremendous sigh. "What in the world are we going to do with all this food?"

Aunt Harriet answered the question. "What we don't use ourselves, we'll freeze."

John laughed. "You know I have a pretty good appetite. I'll help you out a little."

He and the three Danas sat down at the dining room table and ate sandwiches and doughnuts and drank cider. There had been no more callers for treats, probably because word of the fire had spread. Louise and Jean were heartsick that the party had broken up so suddenly. They were also determined to find out who had set the fire!

Harriet Dana looked at her nieces for several seconds. Harriet was a lovely, motherly person who had brought up the girls with the help of her brother Ned, a sea captain. Louise's and Jean's parents had died when the girls were very young. Louise was a pretty, dark-haired seventeen-year-old, and her blonde sister was a year younger.

Miss Dana said, "Perhaps we should call the fire department and the police."

Jean answered, "The fire is out. Why don't we look for more clues ourselves before we contact the authorities?"

The others agreed and started a search in the yard. At first they detected nothing, not even a clear footprint. Too many people had entered and left the house. Finally they approached the street. Two little Halloween ghosts, a girl and a boy, were seated at the end of the driveway.

"Did you have a fire?" the girl asked.

"Yes," Louise replied. "But it's out now. I hope you weren't frightened by it. It's late. Shouldn't you be going home?"

"We're afraid we'll meet the bad men who ran out of your house."

"What bad men?"

"The witch and the scarecrow. We saw them when they ran away."

"Why do you think they're bad men?" Jean asked eagerly.

"Because they told us not to follow them, or we would get hurt," the child replied.

"Which direction did they take?"

"They started down the street, but then they changed their minds and went into the backyard," the little boy said.

The Danas looked at one another, then Aunt Harriet spoke up. "I'm glad you didn't follow. We'll look for them, but you'd better run home now."

The children nodded and left. John and the Danas walked quickly down the driveway. At the back a boxwood hedge separated the adjoining property.

John suddenly stopped. "What's that?"

Jean had already spied a light piece of cloth. She parted the bushes. "Two costumes!" she cried out, picking them up. "Our uninvited guests left their outfits here!"

Beside the witch's tall hat lay the broom he had carried. A note was attached to the handle. Louise hurried into the Danas' garage to get a flashlight, then shone it on the message. It was printed and read:

BEWARE OF THE WITCH'S OMEN. ONLY THE STORM PETREL KNOWS MY SECRET. YOU WILL NEVER FIND ME—BUT YOU AND CAPTAIN DANA WILL HAVE PLENTY OF BAD LUCK!

The Danas and John were puzzled. Was this a Halloween prank, or was there a more sinister meaning to the message?

John asked, "What possible connection could there be between a witch and a bird of the sea?"

No one could answer the question. Jean said, "Uncle Ned will be home soon because his ship, the *Balaska*, is due to dock in New York. We'll ask him about the storm petrel and tell him the whole story. Maybe he can figure it out."

The girls gathered up the costumes and the broom and took them into the house. John went home, but the Danas continued to discuss the strange evening. They came to the conclusion that until they found out whether or not this was a Halloween prank, they would not contact the police.

Louise and Jean were again talking about the mystery at breakfast the following morning when the mail arrived. There was a letter for them that had no sender's name or return address on it. Louise opened it. Inside were two tickets. The word *Complimentary* was stamped on them.

"I wonder who sent these?" she said, surprised.

"What are they for?" Jean asked.

"They're invitations to a private show of unusual birds at the Ornithological Society in the Dawson Library."

"How wonderful!" Jean exclaimed. "Some we'll

recognize, but others might be from foreign places. I'm sure they'll have rare birds that we have never seen before."

"It does sound intriguing," Louise agreed. "I wonder if there'll be any storm petrels at the show." She caught her breath. "Maybe these invitations were sent by the witch!"

Suddenly the sisters wondered if they should use the tickets. If the mysterious witch had sent them, would he be there to cause more mischief?

CHAPTER II

Brazen Theft

LOUISE had an idea. "Jean, why don't we call on our neighbour, Mrs. Harrington? She's a member of the Ornithological Society."

"Good idea!" Jean replied. "Do you want to find out if she sent the tickets?"

"Yes."

The girls hurried down the street. Fortunately, Mrs. Harrington was at home and said she was delighted to see them. Louise and Jean were always fascinated by her house. Stuffed rare birds were standing on tables and cabinets, and she had many live ones in a room upstairs. The sisters had tried to learn the names of them all but had never succeeded.

Jean said, "Mrs. Harrington, Louise and I think we have run into another mystery. Maybe you can help. Did you send us two tickets to the Ornithological Society show in Dawson?"

The woman shook her head. "No, I didn't. But I am glad you have the chance to go. It's really wonderful. All the birds there are alive, and some of them are absolutely exquisite."

Louise said that they had received the two invitations in an unmarked envelope, and she explained what had happened in their home the night before.

Mrs. Harrington was stunned. "A fire!" she exclaimed. "I'd say that's a very sick Halloween joke, indeed. And why that witch called himself 'keeper of the storm petrel' is a mystery to me."

"We don't understand, either," Louise said. "But it's the reason we think he might have sent us the tickets for the show."

"As far as that's concerned," Mrs. Harrington declared, "the show is very well run, and I think you should attend. No one could get away with any mischief there. As a matter of fact, would you like to go with me? I'll try to get another ticket for your Aunt Harriet, if she'd care to join us."

"That would be lovely," Jean said. "We'll ask her."

Mrs. Harrington looked off into space. The girls wondered what she was thinking about. Finally she said, " 'Cruelty ever proceeds from a vile mind, and often from a cowardly heart.' A long time ago a man named Harington—not a relative of mine—said this. How true it is! If I were you girls, I wouldn't worry about the witch. I'd say he is a coward in hiding."

Jean wondered if the witch would be at the show. "We couldn't identify him if he were because his costume really hid him well."

"Maybe you'll recognize his voice," Mrs. Harrington suggested. Then she changed the subject. "I have a stuffed storm petrel here. Would you like to see it?"

"Oh, yes!" the Danas exclaimed.

The woman went upstairs and a few minutes later appeared with a large box. She set it on the dining room table, opened it, and took out a stand on which a storm petrel stood.

"It's a handsome bird," Louise remarked.

"Yes," Mrs. Harrington agreed. "And very smart."

The bird was black and white and about five and a half inches long. Mrs. Harrington reached into the box and removed a photo that showed a storm petrel in flight, gliding gracefully through the air. Its legs were swung back, and the wings, which seemed large for its body, were straight up in the air.

"Is it true," Louise asked, "that the storm petrel can predict bad weather?"

"Indeed it is," Mrs. Harrington answered.

"There are many stories about sailors at sea being warned by such birds to stay out of a storm, and they turned back in time and were saved."

"I'm sure there must have been some who didn't turn back and lost their lives," Jean remarked.

Mrs. Harrington nodded. "Unfortunately, yes." Then she smiled. "The legend I like best is the one about the phantom ship approaching another vessel. The petrels carried on so loudly that the captain decided to take their warning seriously and scooted away from the ghost ship."

Louise laughed. "That sounds like a good Halloween story. 'Halloween on shipboard.' "

After a little more conversation with the friendly bird collector, the girls said they must return home. On the way Jean suggested that one of the many legends about petrels might be a clue to the witch's identity.

"Maybe Uncle Ned will know," Louise replied.

When the Danas entered their house, they found Aunt Harriet extremely agitated.

"What happened?" Louise asked.

"You remember that fine expensive barometer that was hanging on the wall near the coat closet in the hall? It's gone!"

"You mean it was stolen?" Jean asked, shocked.

"I'm afraid so," Aunt Harriet replied. "It's my guess that while Jean was dancing with the witch last night, the scarecrow took the barometer off the wall and hid it under his clothes."

"How terrible!" Jean exclaimed. "That was an heirloom belonging to Uncle Ned, and he just loved it."

Aunt Harriet nodded. The girls examined the place on the wall where the barometer had hung. The thief had even pulled out the hook to which the instrument had been attached.

"I'm going to report this to the police," Aunt Harriet announced. "Too many strange things have happened here lately that I'm sure were more than Halloween pranks!"

The girls agreed. Then Jean suggested that she and Louise go downtown and visit all the antique shops to see if any of them had bought the barometer. "The thief certainly had plenty of time to get rid of it," she remarked.

They hurried off and went from one shop to another. Each time they ended up disappointed. Not one had Uncle Ned's barometer.

As the sisters walked home, they discussed the case from every angle. Finally Louise said, "I believe both of those men are connected with the sea. They are probably sailors. While one was talking about storm petrels, the other was stealing Uncle Ned's barometer."

Jean thought this was an excellent assumption and suggested they examine the men's costumes again. "We may pick up another clue," she added.

When the Danas returned home, they told Aunt Harriet that their search for the barometer had been unsuccessful. "Apparently the thief didn't steal it for its resale value but wanted it for himself," Louise said. When she noticed her aunt's sad face, she added, "But we'll get it back when we find the thief!"

Next the girls went over the costumes minutely. Louise checked the witch's outfit, while Jean checked the scarecrow's. For a few minutes there was silence. Then Jean announced, "I haven't discovered much, but besides being short and heavyset, the scarecrow had dark hair."

"How did you come to that conclusion?" Louise asked curiously.

Jean picked up a black hair from inside the scarecrow's wig. "Here's my evidence."

Louise grinned. "Very good, Sherlock Holmes."

"What about you?" her sister inquired. "Have you noticed anything?"

"Nothing, except that the witch has a large head." Louise put the hat on her head. It came down over her eyes and ears. She giggled. "Look at this."

"It doesn't suit you," Jean admitted.

"We already know the man has large hands and feet," Louise declared, "and he's rather slim and tall. But all this won't do us any good because we can't describe his face!"

"And that goes for the scarecrow, too," Jean added glumly.

The following day Aunt Harriet, her nieces, and Mrs. Harrington went to the Ornithological Society show. The exhibit was in a large room that the library rented out for lectures and dances. The centre of the room was filled with tall plants and small trees, and here and there birds nestled in them, chattering or singing. Along the walls were booths. In them were many cages containing beautiful birds.

"Aren't they magnificent!" Mrs. Harrington exclaimed.

"They certainly are," Louise replied. "And there are lots I have never seen before—not even in pictures."

Mrs. Harrington explained that many had come from the Pacific Islands and parts of South America and Africa where the climate was always warm. She pointed to a bright green bird with a red stomach and commented on the tail feathers, which were at least three times its length. "This is the quetzal," she said. "It's one of the most picturesque birds because of its vivid colours and its long tail."

"I like this black and yellow one with the huge beak," Louise said. "He looks as if he's smoking a cigar."

Mrs. Harrington laughed. "That's a toucan from Central America. I'm sure he's smart enough to know that smoking is hazardous to his health!"

The group chatted gaily and walked past the various booths, each bearing the name and address of the exhibitor. Suddenly Jean stopped short and grabbed Louise's arm. "Over there!" she said, pointing. "That's a live storm petrel!"

The bird sat on a perch. It was attached to the bar by a chain around its right leg.

Mrs. Harrington frowned. "I haven't seen this one before, and I know most of the storm petrels around here. I wonder to whom it belongs."

Louise looked in her programme for Booth 28. It was not listed.

"It could be a late entrant," Mrs. Harrington explained. "Sometimes people sign up after the brochure is printed."

"Let's ask the owner whether he has any more petrels," Jean suggested, and they walked toward the booth.

The man standing near the bird was short, heavyset, and had dark hair and small feet. Louise whispered to Jean, "He's certainly not the witch."

"But he could be the scarecrow!" Jean replied.

Louise stepped up for a closer look at the man. At that instant the petrel dive-bombed toward her face!

CHAPTER III

The Faker

SEVERAL people at the bird show rushed forward to help Louise. After the storm petrel pecked at her, she pulled back enough so he could not reach her any longer. Her face was bleeding in several spots.

Jean stood horrified at her side. "Oh, Louise! How awful! Here, let me help you." She pulled a clean handkerchief from her pocket and began to wipe her sister's face.

Aunt Harriet spoke up. "We must put some antiseptic on those bites right away."

She opened her purse and pulled out a small tube of salve. Quickly she dabbed it on the spots, and at once the stinging stopped.

Jean was angry. She called to the man who owned the bird. "You shouldn't have a dangerous petrel in this show!"

He looked at her solemnly. "Nobody is supposed to get too close."

"Maybe I did come too near the bird," Louise admitted. "But I wanted to talk to you."

"What do you want to know?" the man asked.

"Who are you?" Louise said. "Your name is not in the programme."

"I have a perfect right to be here." He scowled. "It was too late for me to get listed, but the committee knows all about me. Besides, what difference does it make to you? You've got me in trouble already by coming too close to my bird. Who are you, anyway?"

"We're Louise and Jean Dana," Louise replied. "And this is our Aunt Harriet, and Mrs. Harrington, a friend."

"I've never seen you in any of our shows," Mrs. Harrington said to the man. "Do you have many birds?"

"No, just this one."

"Do you own it?" Jean inquired.

"Well, not exactly," the man said. "A friend of mine found it mangled on the beach and asked me if I would take it. I tried to sell it, but the bird is not very friendly, so I guess I won't be able to. Anyway, I've become kind of attached to him."

"You'll keep him, then?"

"I'll let my friend decide."

The crowd that had assembled began to disperse, and the Danas moved off also when the man turned to talk to someone else.

"The petrel owner didn't tell us his name," Louise remarked when they were out of earshot of Booth 28. "I see a policeman over there. Maybe he can get it for us."

She walked up to the officer and asked him.

"I suppose I could find out," he replied. "Why do you want to know?"

The girl pointed to her face. "His bird pecked me repeatedly, and the man was very unfriendly about it, saying it was my own fault."

"In that case I'll be glad to get his name for you," the officer said. "Wait here. I'll be right back."

He was gone only a few minutes, then returned with a piece of paper. "The exhibitor in Booth 28 is Randy Mercek," the officer reported. "He lives at 10 Longwood Street, Johnsville. Here, I wrote it out for you." He handed her the piece of paper.

"Thank you," Louise said. Then she went back to the others. "Aunt Harriet, do you mind if we borrow your car and go to Johnsville? We'd like to find out more about this man."

"Sure, it's not far. You can pick us up on the way back."

Twenty minutes later the girls arrived in the neighbouring town. Jean inquired at the post office where Longwood Street was located.

An official gave her directions, and she went back to the car. "It's in a new development a little way out of town," she told her sister.

Louise, who was driving, followed the instructions. When they reached the spot where number ten should have been, there was nothing but a vacant lot. The girls looked at each other.

"That man gave a phony address on purpose," Jean declared.

"Yes, he did," Louise agreed. "And I wonder if his name really is Randy Mercek."

Disappointed, the Danas rode back to the bird show. They were determined to talk to the man with the petrel and demand the truth. As they neared his booth, Jean stopped suddenly, "Oh no! He's gone! He moved out!"

Louise made a face. "We were pretty stupid not to ask Aunt Harriet and Mrs. Harrington to watch him," she said dejectedly.

Jean agreed. "Now we're right back to zero as far as his identity is concerned. What do we do next?"

At this moment a man walked up to them. "Do you know where the exhibitor of this booth went?"

The girls shook their heads. "We were looking for him ourselves."

"I'm on the committee," the man continued. "I just learned that he was charging fifty cents to anyone who wanted to take his bird's picture. That's against the rules. Our society doesn't permit this kind of thing."

"We checked out the address he gave the Society," Jean said. "It's a vacant lot. He's not honest!"

"You're right," the committeeman said, running his fingers through his hair. "He sneaked in here, and we didn't realize he wasn't on the level." He looked at Louise. "Are you the girl his bird pecked?"

"Yes."

"I'm truly sorry. I guess we weren't alert enough. Are your injuries serious? I mean, are you going to pursue the matter with the Ornithological Society?"

"I don't think so. I'm sure my cuts will heal without complications."

"I'm glad to hear that," the man said, relieved. He turned to walk away, but Louise caught him by the sleeve.

"Do you mind if we investigate Mercek's booth? Perhaps we'll find a clue as to where he really lives."

"Go right ahead. And let me know if you're

successful. I'd like to catch that scoundrel myself!"

The young detectives walked into the small enclosure and kicked aside a carton that had contained food for the petrel.

"I'm surprised he got a booth for his one little bird," Jean said.

Louise nodded. "They must have had one left, or perhaps there was a cancellation." She noticed a piece of scrap torn from a newspaper. Curiously she picked it up and read the item with interest.

"What does it say?" Jean asked.

"It's an ad to send for a book of jokes about sailors," her sister replied. She laughed out loud. "There are a couple right here. Listen to this: Why is a sailor like a tree? Because he has lots of leaves."

Jean made a face. "How corny!"

"Why are monkeys and sailors alike?" Louise read the next joke. "Because both can climb high. The monkey climbs a tree, the sailor climbs a mast."

Jean groaned again. "If all the jokes in the book are that bad, I wouldn't pay much for it."

Louise became serious. "This may be a clue for us, Jean. I'm positive now that Mercek is a sailor. Maybe the witch is, too. They probably were buddies on some ship."

"But why are they our enemies?" Jean asked.

Louise said she felt that the real target of the

men's wrath might be their Uncle Ned Dana. "It's even possible these men once worked on the *Balaska*. Perhaps they were discharged and are trying to get even with the captain."

Jean added. "And they are taking it out on you and me!"

"Exactly. I'll be so glad when Uncle Ned gets here and we can talk to him about it."

Aunt Harriet came up to the girls and said that Mrs. Harrington had bought a rare chicken petrel. "Do come over and look at it."

The girls followed her. Mrs. Harrington had already put the lovely bird into a cage.

When Louise saw it, she laughed. "It really looks like a miniature chicken."

"No," Jean said. "It's prettier."

The Danas dropped Mrs. Harrington and her bird off at her home, then continued to their own house.

The next morning they had just finished breakfast when the telephone rang. Mrs. Harrington was on the line. She was extremely upset and spoke so fast that Louise could hardly understand her.

"Please, Mrs. Harrington," the girl pleaded, "speak a little slower. I can't hear you."

The woman calmed down enough to be intelligible. "Louise! I don't know what to do. That rare, expensive chicken petrel I bought yesterday has mysteriously disappeared!"

CHAPTER IV

Trapped!

"JEAN and I will be right over," Louise promised. "Apparently someone interested in petrels knew the value of your bird and stole it."

She went back to the breakfast table and told her sister and Aunt Harriet what had happened.

"Do you think it was that man who called himself Randy Mercek?" Jean asked.

"I don't know. It's possible. Why don't we go over to Mrs. Harrington's and hunt for a clue?"

"Good idea," Jean said and got up from the table.

When the Danas reached the bird collector's house, they examined the doors and windows to see how the thief had entered. Finally they discovered a cellar window that was not locked.

"He could have let himself in that way," Louise said.

The girls hunted for further clues in the house but found nothing.

"I'm dreadfully sorry that you lost your valuable bird," Louise said to Mrs. Harrington. "But I suppose you're lucky that the thief didn't take any others."

Just then the telephone rang. Mrs. Harrington answered. "Oh, hello, Henry. What's that? Tell me all about it."

There was a rather lengthy pause. Then Mrs. Harrington put down the phone and turned to the girls.

"A friend of mine, Henry Buckle, lives down the street. While I was gone from the house, he happened to be out walking. A man passed him, holding an unusual looking bird. Henry knows that I collect birds and thought this one might possibly belong to me. He said it looked like a chicken!"

"It must have been your stolen petrel!" Louise cried out.

Mrs. Harrington nodded. "Henry ran after the man to ask him where he had obtained the bird. Just then it flew out of the stranger's hands, and although the man tried to capture it again, he was unable to."

"Did Mr. Buckle say which direction the bird took?" Jean inquired.

"Yes, he did," Mrs. Harrington replied. "He said it flew toward the sun."

"That means east," Jean spoke up. "Louise, why don't we get Aunt Harriet's car and see if we can chase the bird?"

Both Mrs. Harrington and Miss Dana felt there was little chance to retrieve the chicken petrel but agreed that the girls could try. The two rode off with Louise behind the wheel. Jean was scanning the sky with a pair of binoculars she had borrowed from her aunt.

They covered several miles. Finally Jean sighed. "That bird could have changed course after the first five minutes of its flight, and we could keep going east until we ride straight into the Atlantic Ocean!"

Louise giggled. "You have a point there. Look what's coming up in the distance."

Jean trained her binoculars on a tall, narrow building. "Oh, the old revolutionary tower," she said.

The Danas knew the historic landmark that had once been part of a stone fort. Now it was the only structure left of the revolutionary site.

"The petrel may have taken refuge in there," Louise suggested. "I'll drive up to it." She left the highway and turned into the small, rutted lane that led to the tower. The building was surrounded by tall grass, weeds, and a few scraggly flowers that struggled for existence.

Jean scanned the tower through her binoculars.

There was no sign of the bird, but suddenly she gasped. A man's hand appeared in one of the openings at the top of the building!

"Louise! Somebody's in there!"

"What!"

"Look up in the middle opening. Here!" Jean handed her sister the binoculars.

Louise stopped the car and peered through the glasses. "He seems to be sprinkling something on the sill," she said. "Maybe he's feeding birds!"

Just then a strange-looking bird that resembled a chicken flew around the tower from the back and settled on the sill, greedily eating the seeds the stranger had sprinkled on it. Quick as a flash, the man's hand reached out again, grabbed the bird's legs, and pulled it inside!

Louise and Jean heard a squawking sound, then the bird disappeared from sight.

"That poor thing!" Louise exclaimed. "I'll bet it's Mrs. Harrington's petrel. Let's go in and try to rescue it!"

"Right. Why don't you park next to those bushes over there?"

Louise did, and the two girls went up to the tower. Jean knocked on the door. No one answered. She tried the knob. The door was locked.

Jean walked back a few steps and called out, "Hello up there! Please open the door!" Still there was no response.

"I'm sure that man heard us," she declared. "Why won't he let us in?"

"Maybe he has something to hide. Besides, he may not want us to see the bird. Perhaps he knows what it's worth and will try to sell it!"

As the Danas stood wondering what to do, a door slammed.

"There must be another entrance to the tower," Jean cried out. "Let's look for it!"

The girls circled the building. At the rear they discovered a trapdoor hidden by tall grass.

"This must be what we heard!" Louise said.

"Most likely," her sister agreed, pointing to a path of freshly trampled grass leading away from the trapdoor.

"Someone just came out of here," she declared. "See how the blades are bent all the way down? And the steps are short, which means he was in a hurry."

"Perhaps we can still catch him!" Louise said excitedly. "Come on!"

The trail led to a tumbledown building and continued on the other side for a short distance before ending at the road. There was no one in sight, and too many vehicle tracks crisscrossed the rutted lane for any human footprints to be visible among them.

"We lost our suspect!" Jean said with a sigh.

"Let's go back and see if that trapdoor is open," Louise suggested.

To their delight, the girls found the door unlocked. Louise pulled on the handle, and Jean peered into the opening.

A flight of narrow stone steps led down to a darkened area, but to their surprise, a lighted lantern hung next to the entrance.

Louise opened the door all the way, and the girls slipped inside. Jean picked up the lantern. "This must be what the man used," she said with a grin. "Now it's our turn!"

Holding it high, she led the way to the bottom of the steps. A long black tunnel lay before them. After walking through it, they went up another flight of stairs that ended at a door. Louise pushed it open. The door squeaked loudly.

The girls found themselves in the empty rotunda of the tower. An iron ladder extended to the top. Quickly the sisters climbed up into a good-sized room.

It contained a cot, a few empty food cans, and birdseed scattered on the floor and the lookouts. Louise stepped up to one of them.

"I suppose this is where the revolutionary soldiers put their muskets and fired at the enemy," she surmised. "It's a horrible thought."

Jean agreed. "Personally, I think this place makes a wonderful bird sanctuary," she added, changing the subject. "I wonder who is staying here."

"Maybe a caretaker," Louise suggested.

Jean shook her head. "If someone lived here all the time, he'd have more furniture."

The Danas continued to speculate about the stranger and the stolen chicken petrel.

"The thief might be a friend of the tower man!" Louise surmised.

Jean laughed. "So he told the bird before it flew away to stop here and visit his buddy."

"I guess you're right. It's too far-fetched."

"If the tower man was in league with anybody, I would think he'd have some means of communication here. But there's no telephone, no shortwave radio, no C.B. I think he's just a hermit," Jean said.

Louise smiled. "He could have used carrier pigeons to deliver messages!"

"There's no sign of that, either."

The girls examined each opening but discovered nothing to help them answer their questions. At last Jean said, "We may as well leave."

The two detectives descended the ladder to the rotunda and opened the door to the tunnel. Just then the light in their lantern went out! At the same moment a door slammed shut, and they heard a bolt fall into place.

"Jean! We're locked in!" Louise cried out in panic.

"Let's not jump to conclusions," Jean said, trying to sound calm. "Maybe it wasn't the trapdoor at all."

Frightened, the sisters stumbled through the dirt passageway. Cobwebs cut across their faces, and it suddenly occurred to them how musty the tunnel was. They felt their way along the dusty walls until they reached the end, then climbed the steps to the trapdoor. Louise attempted to open it.

The door would not budge!

"Let me try," Jean said anxiously.

But she had no better luck. Even when the two girls pushed together with all their might, the bolt did not give.

"Louise," Jean said finally. "It's hopeless. We're locked in!"

CHAPTER V

The Black Tunnel

EXHAUSTED from their struggle to open the trapdoor, Louise and Jean sank down on the stone steps.

"What'll we do now?" Jean wailed.

Louise did not reply. Suddenly she stood up. "I have a vague recollection of a kerosene can standing against one of the walls in the tunnel. Let's take the lantern and try to find it."

The girls climbed down the stairs and separated, each moving along one wall. They shuffled their feet in order not to miss the can. Finally Louise located it. She bent down and sniffed.

"It *is* kerosene!" she called out triumphantly. "Do you have the lantern?"

"Right here." Jean made her way over to her sister, and they filled the empty container.

"There's one little thing we forgot," Jean said suddenly. "We need matches!"

Louise groaned. "You're right. I believe there's a shelf on this wall. I'll see if there are any matches on it." She felt her way along the wall until her fingers touched the shelf. A few seconds later she cried out in glee. "I found some. Now we're okay!"

Fortunately, the book of matches was almost full. Louise struck one. It went out instantly. She tried another. This one would not even light up.

"The matches are damp," she said, not daring to think that none of them would work. She used a third, trying to guard the spark by holding her hand over it. But it was in vain.

Finally Jean said, "I have an idea. Let me have the matches."

She took a clean handkerchief from her pocket, then tore a match out of the book. Carefully she patted it dry, and wiped off the rough part of the book on which she would light the match. Satisfied that it was much dryer now, she tried again. This time she succeeded!

Louise said, "Pretty smart."

Jean nodded. "Now we can light the lantern, but we still have to figure out how to get out of this place!"

They tried the front door of the tower, but it was nailed shut, and there was not a single tool with which to open it!

"Let's play revolutionary soldier," Jean suggested. "We'll climb to the top of the tower and swing the lantern out one of those openings. Hopefully someone will see it and rescue us."

"Good idea," Louise said. "Come on."

Up the ladder they went, and they took turns swinging the lantern. It was tiring, and time dragged endlessly.

"And all that this character who stays here has around are empty cans," Louise muttered. "Not a bit of food, and I'm starved!"

Hours passed, and the sun began to set on the horizon. Back at the Dana home, Aunt Harriet was in a panic. She had expected the girls long before this and finally called the police.

After she explained what had happened, the officer in charge tried to calm her. "We know about the stolen bird," he said, "and we'll send out a couple of men right away to locate your nieces."

"They drove in an easterly direction this morning," Aunt Harriet said.

"Right. I'll also alert the state police along the highway to be on the lookout."

"Thank you," Aunt Harriet said. "And please, call me right away when you find them!"

Two officers named Black and Roth set off at once. By the time they had driven past the town limits, it was getting dark. They stopped at petrol stations and roadside restaurants to inquire about Jean and Louise, but to no avail.

"Can you believe all this was caused by a bird?" Black asked. "I sure hope we find those girls."

"So do I," Roth agreed. "Hey, what's that flickering light over there?"

Black pulled to the shoulder of the road, and they both watched the strange signal. "It seems to be coming from the old revolutionary tower," Black said finally. "We've just passed the road to it, but I'll back up."

He turned on his siren to warn travellers and quickly found the entrance to the rutted lane leading to the old structure.

As they approached the tower, Roth cried out, "It's definitely a signal. Somebody's up there. Maybe the Dana girls!"

Black parked the car, and the men jumped out. Jean and Louise had heard the siren and realized that rescue was finally coming.

"Oh, thank goodness!" Louise said with a sigh. She rubbed her arm, which was sore from holding the lantern.

As the men scrambled through the tall grass and weeds with their flashlights, Jean called down to them. "We're Louise and Jean Dana. We're trapped in here!"

Black replied, "We're glad we found you. Your aunt is very worried."

"I don't blame her," Jean said. "There's a trapdoor at the rear of the tower. It's locked from the outside. We'll come down to meet you."

While the officers were prising the trapdoor open, the young detectives descended the ladder and scooted across the rotunda. They reached the stairway leading down into the tunnel when the two officers walked up to them.

"Are you all right?" Black asked anxiously.

"Yes, and relieved to see you!" Louise replied.

Jean told what had happened and how the girls had discovered the lantern, the kerosene, and the matches.

"They were a life saver," she added.

"You actually saw the chicken petrel fly into one of the openings?" Roth questioned.

"Yes," Louise replied and explained about the cot in the tower room and the scattered birdseed. "By the time we got here, though, the petrel and the man were gone. We believe he drove away but came back a little later to lock us in," she added.

The men nodded. Officer Black said, "Roth, suppose you and I climb up there and take a look ourselves. I'd like to know if somebody is camping out here."

"I'm sure someone is," Jean spoke up. "We found empty food cans."

After the two men had inspected the tower

room, they decided to stay and watch the place. "Maybe we can nab the inhabitant and find out what happened to the chicken petrel," Roth said as they all went back through the tunnel.

Louise hung up the lantern where she had found it, leaving it lighted. Then they climbed out of the trapdoor, closed it behind them, and walked to the Dana car. The officers promised to get in touch with them if the stranger should return to the tower.

"In the meantime," Roth said, "I'll telephone headquarters and ask them to notify your aunt that you're safe and on your way home."

"Oh, thank you," both girls said as they climbed into their car and set off.

"Let's stop at the next hamburger place," Jean suggested. "I don't think I'll last till we get home."

Louise chuckled. "Neither will I."

When they reached the Dana house an hour later, Aunt Harriet hugged them in relief. "I'm glad you're here!" she said. "I was so worried."

"We didn't mean to give you such a scare," Louise said, "but we were locked in."

"I know. A man from headquarters called and told me all about it. By the way, you'd better give Mrs. Harrington a call. She'd like to know what you found out."

Louise did, and the bird collector was relieved that the girls were safe. But she was upset when she heard what trouble they had gone through to find the chicken petrel. "I'm glad the police are keeping watch for that man," she declared. "However, the main thing is that nothing happened to you!"

The Danas did not hear from the two officers until the following morning, when Black reported that the man had returned to the tower and had been arrested for trespassing.

"He refused to give his name but admitted that he fed birds. He insists, however, that they were only pigeons who stopped there off and on. He's a vagrant who thought the tower was a good place to stay."

"He said nothing about taking in a chicken petrel?" Louise inquired.

"No. He denied it vehemently. Why don't you girls come over here and talk to him? Maybe you can get more out of him than we could."

When Louise and Jean arrived at the jail, they found that the prisoner was old, with gray hair and a long beard.

"I'm a wanderer," he said sullenly. "Right now I have no job."

Jean shot a question at him. "Are you a friend of Randy Mercek's?"

The man looked blank. "Never heard of him."

Louise spoke up. "My sister and I were watching the tower yesterday. We saw you catch a bird that had been stolen from a friend of ours."

The prisoner became angry. Whether or not he was really insulted or just trying to pretend innocence, the girls could not tell. "I don't know what you're talking about," he stormed. "I certainly didn't pull in any bird!"

"After we entered the tower, did you close the trapdoor behind us from the outside?" Jean asked.

"I never saw you before in my life," the prisoner grumbled. "I closed the door when I went out, but I didn't know anyone was inside the building."

Further questioning revealed nothing, so Louise and Jean left the jail. They had a strong hunch the man was not telling the truth.

"If the prisoner isn't a friend of Mercek, but caught the chicken petrel, where would he have taken it?" Jean asked.

Louise grinned. "I get it. To the pet shop."

"Let's go there and see if by any chance they bought it," Jean suggested, and the two girls hurried off. They greeted the owner and inquired whether a rare chicken petrel had been brought in the previous day.

"As a matter of fact, yes," the man replied. "Yesterday afternoon a man sold one to me. I had it no longer than an hour when another fellow came in to get some bird food. When he spied the rare bird, he was absolutely delighted and purchased it at once."

"I'm sure the petrel was stolen from Mrs. Harrington," Louise declared. "Can you describe the man who sold it to you, and the one who bought it?"

"The seller was an old fellow, with gray hair and a long beard," the store owner replied. "The one who bought the petrel was tall and thin and had a rather hard face."

The girls were sure the old man was the tower dweller. The buyer might have been the witch! "Have you ever seen either of these people before?" Jean asked.

The pet shop owner shook his head. "They were strangers to me. The old man who brought the bird in said he was selling it for a woman who could no longer take care of it. The other guy told me nothing."

"And you have no idea where he went or where he lives?"

"None. But if you'll give me your name and phone number, I'll be glad to contact you if he comes in again."

The girls thanked him and left the store after giving the pet shop owner the information. On their way home, Louise said to Jean, "Do you suppose that by some chance that old tower is a secret meeting place for a gang of some sort?"

Jean said she did not know what to think. The place certainly did not look as if people came and went regularly.

"Also," she added, "why would the tower man

sell the bird to the pet store for the witch to buy if he knew him? He would have just turned it over to him. I'm inclined to think the vagrant doesn't know any of the petrel gang. When the bird flew near the window, he realized its value, caught it, and sold it."

"I guess you're right," Louise agreed. "The witch just happened to go into the pet store at the right time to get hold of the petrel."

The girls had little to say on the trip home. Just as they pulled into the driveway, Louise remarked, "I can't help but put two things together—the witch buying the bird and the warning that we Danas are supposed to have bad luck!"

CHAPTER VI

Hurricane Worries

AUNT Harriet and her nieces were seated in the Dana living room discussing the case.

"None of the pieces of the puzzle seem to fit together," Miss Dana said. The girls agreed.

"I wish one really great clue would turn up," Jean remarked. "Then we could dig into it. Everything so far seems to come to a dead end."

At this moment the young woman who did domestic work for them, Cora Appel, facetiously nicknamed "Applecore" by Jean, rushed into the room. "Oh, oh!" she exclaimed, then tripped, stumbled, and fell flat.

Louise and Jean hurried to help her up and asked if she had hurt herself.

"No," Cora said, then added wildly, "but Captain Dana is in great trouble!"

"What are you talking about?" Aunt Harriet

stared at her. "Where did you hear such a thing?"

"On the radio," Cora replied.

Louise said, "*Exactly* what did you hear?"

Cora replied that Captain Dana's ship, the *Balaska*, had run into a terrible hurricane. "People got washed overboard and everything!" the girl cried.

The Danas knew that Cora tended to exaggerate at times. All of them wondered if this was the case now. They decided to run into the kitchen to listen for themselves. It seemed that Cora had heard the news correctly. Fifty foot waves were reported, and many people were injured. A sailor had indeed been washed overboard.

"This is dreadful!" Aunt Harriet exclaimed.

Jean waved for her to continue listening, but there was no further news about the *Balaska*.

"I'm going to call the steamship office in New York City and find out what happened," Aunt Harriet announced, and hurried to the telephone. The line was busy, however. Anxiously Miss Dana tried again a few seconds later but still had no luck getting through.

Suddenly Cora put a hand to her mouth. "Oh!" she cried and turned on her heels. She rushed to the oven and pulled the door open.

"It's ruined! It's ruined!" she wailed.

"What's ruined?"

"My casserole! I only meant to warm it, but

now it's burned. When I heard about Captain Dana, I forgot all about it! Oh, oh!"

Aunt Harriet tried to soothe the flustered girl, even though she was extremely upset about her brother. Cora, still beside herself, picked up a carton of milk from the table and put it into the oven. As she was about to close the door, Louise dashed over and took it out again.

"Cora, what did you do that for?" she asked.

Poor Cora shook her head in despair. "I don't know. I'm all confused and so worried and—"

Her jabber was interrupted by another report on the radio. The hurricane was increasing. Captain Dana had tried to run out of the storm but had been unable to do so. The tremendous winds had carried one of the lifeboats overboard, injuring a seaman who had attempted to rescue it.

Aunt Harriet started for the telephone. "I'm going to try the steamship line again."

This time her call went through and a man answered.

"Please," Aunt Harriet begged, "I'm Captain Dana's sister. You must tell me—"

The crisp answer was, "The number has been changed. Please call 227–1178."

With trembling hands, Miss Dana dialled the new number. She was told that the story on the radio was, indeed, true. There had been many injuries on board.

"And what's more," the spokesman for the company continued, "Captain Dana is being blamed for not avoiding the hurricane. He will be brought up on charges of gross negligence and incompetence!" The speaker hung up.

Louise and Jean, who had been standing close enough to their aunt to overhear the conversation, were shocked. Tears welled up in their eyes.

"It can't be true!" Jean exclaimed.

"No," Louise agreed. "Uncle Ned is one of the finest navigators on the whole Atlantic Ocean. I wonder if there has been some trouble on board ship? Maybe the crew won't respond to his commands!"

Aunt Harriet added, "It might even be the passengers. Sometimes, when they get very frightened, they go berserk!"

The Danas tried to decide what to do, while Cora was walking around the kitchen, mumbling and wringing her hands. Just then the telephone rang.

Louise answered it. The caller was Mrs. Harrington. She was so upset Louise could hardly understand what she was saying.

"You and Jean—come over here at once!" Louise figured out. "I have a terrible crisis!"

The girl promised to leave immediately and hung up, consternation on her face. "Mrs. Harrington is in trouble," she announced. "We'll have to see her right away!"

Aunt Harriet nodded. "Go ahead. Cora and I'll stay here and monitor the radio in case there is any more news."

The girls hurried outside. Jean said, "What do you think could have happened to Mrs. Harrington?"

Louise shrugged. "I have no idea. But today doesn't seem to be anybody's day. Bad news everywhere."

Soon the sisters arrived at the bird collector's home. She led them straight into the room where she kept her prize birds. The girls stopped short at the door and gasped.

The room was a mess. Empty cages were lying on the floor, small pieces of furniture were turned over, and bird feathers were scattered on the carpet. Two potted plants had been knocked over, spilling dirt and broken leaves. The birds whose cages were still intact were screeching and jabbering in a frightened crescendo.

"Mrs. Harrington, what happened?" Jean asked.

"Cats!" the woman replied. "Cats did this!"

Louise put an arm around her. "Please calm down and tell us about it."

Mrs. Harrington sank into a chair and explained that she had gone to an engagement party that afternoon. "I locked the house securely. But someone broke in and left three vicious cats in this room!"

Jean asked, "The cats were here when you came back?"

"Yes. They mauled some of my rare, priceless birds. And my three petrels are missing!"

Louise and Jean looked at each other. Was Mrs. Harrington trying to tell them that the intruder stole three birds and left the cats to maul others?

"Did you call the police?" Louise inquired.

"Oh, yes. As soon as I walked into the house, those cats tried to attack me. I rushed to my bedroom phone and notified the police. They came and took the cats away."

"Did they look around for clues?" Jean asked.

"Yes, indeed. But they didn't find anything. Oh dear! I'm afraid that the birds that weren't attacked may have been so frightened that they'll die of shock!"

Jean suggested that the cats might provide a clue to the intruder.

"They're gone," Mrs. Harrington said. "When the officers carried the animals outside, they wriggled out of the men's arms and ran away. Oh, they were dreadful cats! They spat and meowed, and one jumped right up toward my face. It was awful!"

"I'm so sorry about the whole thing," Louise said. "Jean and I will do all we can to try to solve the mystery. Tell me, why do you think the intruder brought those cats in here?"

It took a while for Mrs. Harrington to calm down enough to tell them what she suspected.

Finally she said, "Since the only birds taken were the petrels, I believe whoever broke in here is interested in that kind of bird."

"But why the cats?" Jean asked.

"I suppose the thief wanted to scare me enough so I wouldn't go to the police. I really don't know. Oh, what'll I do?"

The girls noticed that more than three cages were empty. Louise asked what happened to those birds.

Mrs. Harrington was on the verge of tears. "They were horribly mangled. The officers said that they would bury them."

Louise and Jean did not know how to help Mrs. Harrington. They finally asked if they could clean up the mess.

Mrs. Harrington shook her head. "I'll do it. But perhaps you can find a clue the police missed."

The girls began a close investigation of the house to see how the intruder had come in. They found that one of the kitchen windows had a hole cut in the glass pane. Apparently he had put his hand through it, unlocked the window, and raised it.

"The thief must have had the cats in a bag or container," Jean said to Louise. "But what a horrible, mean thing to do!"

Louise nodded. "I hope they gave him a few scratches, too!"

The young detectives went back to the bird room and examined each cage, particularly those that had contained the petrels. At first they saw nothing unusual, but finally Louise, who was checking a cage that was lying on the floor, called out, "Jean, come here! I've found something!"

CHAPTER VII

Loop Clue

"WHAT did you discover, Louise?" Jean asked her sister as she hurried to her side.

"This!" Louise replied. She pointed to one of the bars of the empty cage. Dangling from it was a leather circlet with a broken buckle.

"What is it?"

"Let's ask Mrs. Harrington!"

Louise called to the woman who came quickly. "You found a clue?" she asked eagerly.

"Perhaps," Jean replied. "Have you any idea what this is for?"

Mrs. Harrington looked at the leather loop, took it into her hands and frowned. "It certainly has nothing to do with the cage. The man who stole the petrels must have lost it!"

There was silence for several seconds, then Mrs.

Harrington snapped her fingers. "I have it! My husband had something like this. It was attached to a belt loop on his trousers, and he carried keys on it."

She smiled, and a faraway look came into her eyes. "He started using this when he was a sailor in the Navy, and became so fond of it he wore it most of the time."

Louise said, "Mr. Harrington was a sailor?"

The woman nodded.

"Then the person who took the petrels could be a sailor, too!"

"Indeed he could."

Suddenly the three looked at one another. Jean said, "Petrel—sailor—the witch!"

"Or Mercek," Louise added. "Let's hunt for the keys that might have been attached to the leather circlet."

The group spread out and searched. They examined the floor thoroughly and found several keys scattered on the carpet.

"Either the thief doesn't know he lost them," Louise reasoned, "or he didn't have time to pick them up. Maybe something scared him out of the house."

"Probably the first," Jean said, "because Mrs. Harrington didn't come home until his horrible cats had made a mess of this room."

Mrs. Harrington examined the keys closely.

"This one looks just like a key my husband had for his footlocker," she declared.

"Which reinforces our assumption that the thief is a sailor," Jean said.

Louise had a suggestion. "Why don't we watch the lost and found column in the newspaper? The intruder may think he dropped his keys on the street and may advertise. If he gives an address and phone number, we'll find out who he is!"

"Good idea," Jean agreed. "Do you think we should take the keys to the police?"

"Yes," Louise said and put in a call to headquarters. She told Captain Murphy that they had found the keys and suspected the thief who had let the cats into Mrs. Harrington's house had lost them. "We'll bring them right over," she added.

"Good work," the officer complimented her. "We appreciate your help."

Louise and Jean said good-bye to Mrs. Harrington, then went home and asked their aunt if they could borrow the car. They told her about their find and said they wanted to take the keys to the police.

"Have you heard any more about the *Balaska?*" Louise inquired.

Aunt Harriet shook her head. "I tried the steamship line again, but the phones were busy. Perhaps by the time you get back I'll have some news."

Cora still had the kitchen radio on but had

heard nothing more about the hurricane. She complained, "We get more information about people that land on the moon!"

The girls laughed, admitting she was right. Then they set off for headquarters. Captain Murphy praised them for their detective work. "We'll all watch the paper," he said. "If someone advertises and we ask him to come in, you can listen and identify the voice."

"If there's nothing in the paper, but you should get a call, would you let us know immediately?" Jean asked.

"I certainly will," the captain replied.

The girls went home. This time Aunt Harriet did have news. She and Cora looked extremely worried. "I finally got through to the steamship office at the new number," Miss Dana reported. "A man said that the wind had abated somewhat but that it was raining in torrents. And what's worse is that another hurricane is heading in the direction of the *Balaska!*"

"Oh, no!" Jean exclaimed.

Aunt Harriet grimaced. "That fellow I spoke to was pretty rude. He said, 'I hope Captain Dana has sense enough to get out of its way.' Then he hung up."

"Did he give you his name?" Jean asked.

"No. I asked for the president, but he said Commodore Cooke was not in his office. Oh, if there is another hurricane, the ship might even sink!"

Cora Appel burst into tears.

"Crying won't help the situation," Aunt Harriet said nervously.

"B-b-but I can't help it!" Cora sobbed. "Oh dear, I must do something for the captain. He's so nice to me, even when he teases me. I know what I'll do. I'll knit him a sweater. Who knows? He may come home with pneumonia and need it!"

Despite the gravity of the situation, the Danas could not refrain from smiling. Cora certainly did come up with some funny ideas.

After they had gone into the living room, Cora decided to bake a cake first. She mixed the dough with great determination, and everything looked fine as the pan went into the oven. Then the young woman picked up her knitting bag, which she always carried with her. It contained a large ball of dark blue yarn.

"This is a good colour for Captain Dana," she thought, pulling out her needles to begin her task. She started out with the correct number of stitches. Then, after the first few rows, her mind wandered to Uncle Ned. She pictured the *Balaska* tossing helplessly among skyrocketing waves, and the captain unable to command his crew. Cora shivered and her eyes clouded over.

Suddenly an acrid smell drifted from the oven.

Cora dropped her knitting, dashed across the room, and opened the door. The top of the cake was burned black!

The girl grabbed a mitten, put it on, and pulled the pan from the stove. "Oh, dear!" she cried. "I can't seem to do anything right today!" She put the cake on the table and stared at it, her mood blacker than the crust.

At that moment, Jean came into the kitchen. "Do I smell something burning?"

Cora pointed to the cake. "It's hopeless," she mumbled, and walked back to resume her knitting. Now she discovered another mistake. "I purled when I should have knit, and I knit when I should have purled!"

Jean put an arm around the distraught young woman. "I'm afraid you can't do anything about the cake, but you can rip out the stitches in the sweater and start over again." She grinned at Cora. "I'll promise not to tell Uncle Ned what happened."

This remark made Cora feel better. She unravelled her knitting and wound up the wool.

Jean took another look at the cake, then picked up a knife and skimmed off the burned top. She deftly turned the cake upside down and cut out a small piece to eat.

"Why, Cora," she said, "this is delicious! I tell you what. I'll ice it for you."

"Oh, will you?" Cora said. "I'll peel some potatoes and start supper."

Although Aunt Harriet and her nieces tried several more times to get in touch with the steamship office, there was no answer. Hours later they decided it was hopeless and went to bed.

The following morning Jean was the first one up. Quickly she put on her bathrobe and slippers, hurried down to the front hall, and opened the door. The morning paper lay there. She scooped it up and turned eagerly to the *Lost and Found* column.

She ran her finger along the lines, then suddenly stopped at one item:

LOST: SET OF KEYS. PHONE 221–9529.

Waving the paper, Jean hurried back upstairs and woke her sister and Aunt Harriet. "It's here!" she cried out.

"What is?" Louise asked, rubbing her eyes.

"The person who lost his keys has given his phone number!"

The three dressed quickly, then Louise telephoned Mrs. Harrington. She said that as soon as they had finished breakfast, they would pick her up and go to headquarters to listen when the police called the designated number.

"I do hope he's our man," Jean said on the way.

"After all, there's the possibility some innocent person lost a set of keys and put this ad in the paper."

"Think positively," Louise advised.

The group arrived at headquarters, where Captain Murphy already had several newspapers spread out in front of him. "I was waiting for you. If you hadn't walked in now, I would have called you. Let me phone the number."

The visitors picked up extension phones so they could hear the reply. A man's voice, strong and clear, answered. "Hello?"

"This is Captain Murphy. You put an ad in the paper about lost keys?"

"Yes."

"We have a set here at police headquarters. It was found yesterday afternoon."

"I'll come over at once and see if they're mine," the stranger declared and hung up.

The captain turned to the listeners. "Did any of you recognize the voice?"

"He could have been the witch, but I'm not sure," Jean said.

"That's disappointing. But perhaps you can identify the man when he arrives."

Fifteen minutes later a small boy walked through the door. He had bright red hair, and his clothes looked as if he had been wearing them a long time.

He went up to the desk. "I want to pick up the keys you found."

"You?" the captain said. "The man who lost them said he was coming to police headquarters himself."

The urchin looked a bit frightened. "He—he's an invalid. He can't come himself. He asked me to pick them up for him."

"I'm sorry, but I can only give the keys to the owner. He'll have to get here somehow," Captain Murphy replied, "or perhaps a policeman could deliver the keys to his home. Why don't you give me his address and I'll arrange to send someone there."

The little boy was disappointed but said, "I don't know his address, but I will give him the message and he can call you."

The boy then dashed out of the room. As he hurried off, Jean said, "Let's follow him and see where he goes!"

The captain agreed. "There's certainly something strange about this. The man didn't say he was an invalid when he called. I can't leave here, but I'll send an officer with you. Please wait just a second and I'll see who is available to accompany you."

He made a quick phone call, and a plainclothesman named Sloan walked into the office. Then he, Mrs. Harrington, and the Danas hurried downstairs, crowded into Aunt Harriet's car, and drove off with Louise at the wheel. They could see the red-haired boy hurrying down the street, and they began their pursuit!

CHAPTER VIII

Ambushed Detective

THE red-haired boy was fleet-footed. He dashed down the street and disappeared in an alleyway. Those in the Dana car, pursuing him, were nonplussed. What should they do now?

Detective Sloan said, "I know where this alley ends. Drive around the block, and I'll show you."

Louise did, but before they reached the spot, the urchin had hurried out and turned to the right. In a few moments, he disappeared into another alley.

By the time the Danas and their companions got to the other side of it, the boy was nowhere in sight. Louise pulled over to the curb, opened the window, and called out to a passerby. "Did you see a red-haired boy running out of this alley?"

"Yes."

"Where did he go?"

"Down the street and around the corner."

"Thank you."

Louise set off again. Soon they saw the urchin in the distance. He walked toward a rundown apartment house and seconds later disappeared inside.

Detective Sloan asked Louise to stop, and he jumped out of the car in a flash. He ran after the boy, while Louise parked on the opposite side of the building to get a better view of it. To everyone's surprise, the boy came out of the door a few minutes later, but the detective was not with him.

"Shall we follow him?" Louise asked.

"Wait," Jean said, watching the urchin join a group of children heading for a neighbourhood playground.

"I think he did his errand and is now off with his friends," Jean said. "Let's wait for the detective."

Half an hour passed, and Mrs. Harrington began to fidget. "Why is he taking so long?" she asked.

Louise was concerned. "If he doesn't show up pretty soon, I'm going in to see why."

"Good idea," Jean agreed. "I don't trust that man who phoned. Anything could have happened to Detective Sloan. Let's go now!"

"Shall I wait here?" Mrs. Harrington asked.

"Yes," Jean replied. "Why don't you watch the building and let us know if you see anything suspicious."

The sisters walked into the apartment house and

began to knock on doors. "Did you advertise because you lost your keys?" they asked the various tenants. Each time the reply was no. Some people did not come to the door, and the girls assumed they were out.

Jean was about to ascend to the second floor when Louise held her back. "This may not be a smart thing to do. We may run into the same trouble Detective Sloan evidently did. Why don't we call headquarters and ask them to send us some help?"

Jean agreed, and the two returned to the street. Not far from their parked car was a telephone booth. Louise went in and dialled headquarters. Captain Murphy answered.

"This is Louise Dana," the girl said, then told him of their worries about Detective Sloan. "Could you send another officer over here?" she inquired.

"Sure. Where are you?"

Louise gave him the address and said she and Jean would wait in front of the apartment house. They hurried to their post. Still there was no sign of the detective, but minutes later two police officers arrived. The girls went into the building with them and questioned people on the second floor. All replies were negative.

On the third floor none of the tenants answered their bells. Suddenly they heard a low, threatening voice through one of the doors.

"You squeal, and I'll finish you!"

There was no reply.

Jean whispered, "The speaker sounds like the witch!"

The police officers knocked and demanded to be admitted in the name of the law. There was no answer, but they heard a feeble cry. Finally the officers forced the door open.

Detective Sloan was lying on the floor, bound and gagged!

He was chained to a heavy table leg and looked at them helplessly. While the officers untied him, Jean and Louise ran through the apartment to search for his attacker. There was no sign of him, but an open window next to a fire escape indicated that he had left that way.

"I wonder who he was," Louise said. "Let's look around for clues to his identity."

They returned to the front room just in time to hear Sloan's story. He had seen the red-haired boy run from the apartment, and he rang the bell. The door was opened, and he was instantly attacked by two men.

"You see what they did to me," he added. "I never had a chance to defend myself. Apparently the boy had a hunch he was being followed and warned them. They were furious that we refused to give him the keys."

Louise asked, "Did you find out anything from your attackers?"

Sloan shook his head. "One of them left immediately, saying he'd go out the back door. He was heavyset and short, with dark hair."

"He must have been Randy Mercek!" Jean said.

Sloan nodded, then went on with his story. "The other fellow was tall and slender and had a hard face. You'll have to watch out for him."

"Why? Did he say something about us?" Louise asked.

"Yes. He asked if I was working for the Danas. I didn't answer, and he went on, 'Well, you'd better quit, or they'll get hurt!'" The detective asked the girls what the man had meant by this.

Jean told him what happened on Halloween night when the witch had left the strange message. "We've been threatened since," she added, "but we have no idea why. Maybe we're in their way for some reason, and they'll harm us whenever they get a chance."

Detective Sloan was worried. "You should give up working on the mystery," he suggested.

The girls were shocked at this remark and shook their heads. Jean said, "Not us! We won't give up until it's solved!"

The other two policemen laughed. "Girls with grit," one of them said. "I like that. Can you tell us any more about this?"

Jean smiled. "We looked around the apartment. The man who lives here is fond of petrels. There are several cages in the kitchen."

The group followed her curiously to see the birds.

"Unusual," the policeman said. "I've seen black and white storm petrels, but I've never seen any like these."

"One of them looks like a chicken," Detective Sloan chuckled.

"Our friend Mrs. Harrington owned several such birds, among them a chicken petrel," Jean said. "I believe these may be hers. She's downstairs waiting in the car for us. I'll bring her up here to see if she can identify these birds."

While Jean was gone, the others searched the apartment, looking for clues to the tenant. But none had been found by the time Jean and Mrs. Harrington came in.

The bird collector was led into the kitchen. She walked up to the cages and called out, "Oh, these are mine! These three are the ones that were stolen from my house yesterday, and here's my chicken petrel, too! These other birds must belong to the thief."

She gazed fondly at the birds that chirped and fluttered as if they recognized her. "The poor things!" Mrs. Harrington said. "They've certainly been neglected. They need food and water, and the cages must be cleaned!"

Everyone looked around for seeds, and Jean found a packet. As she sprinkled some into the birds' cups and gave them water, Detective Sloan asked Mrs. Harrington if she knew what kind of petrels they were.

"Oh, yes," she answered. "This is a diving petrel, and this lovely bird is a shearwater. There's a story that claims that it, like a swan, may sing just before it dies. Of course, there are very few of these birds in captivity, so it's hard to prove the story."

The petrels were paying no attention to the visitors. Some were eating, others were chirping happily.

"Obviously it was the owner of this apartment who let the cats loose in my house!" Mrs. Harrington declared. "Oh, I hope he comes back soon so you can arrest him."

"He knows we're after him," Detective Sloan said. "There's a good chance he won't return."

"In that case, I'd be happy to take care of all these birds," Mrs. Harrington offered. "I assume I can take my own birds home right away?"

"I think so," one of the policemen replied. "You reported them stolen, and they were found. No problem."

Louise and Jean continued their search of the apartment. The others joined them, and while Detective Sloan pulled out bureau drawers, the two officers investigated bedroom closets.

Jean was checking a small wooden jewel box. It had several drawers. She pulled one out.

"Here's something!" she exclaimed. "It's a membership card in a seaman's association."

The others came to look at it, and Sloan asked, "What does it say?"

"It was issued to a man named Emil Yansky," Jean replied.

"Emil Yansky?" the detective repeated. "Do you suppose that's the real name of the witch?"

The Danas were inclined to think so, and Louise said, "Now we have something to go on!"

On the card was a snapshot of the man and a date. Jean took a few seconds to decipher it. Apparently the card had been carried loose, and the number was almost rubbed off.

"It's ten years old," she said finally.

There was no need for the group to stay in the apartment any longer. One of the officers closed and locked the window to the fire escape. The other said he would remain on guard in case Yansky returned.

Detective Sloan turned to Louise. "May I have Yansky's card? I'd like to take it to headquarters and look through our files. Perhaps we have a dossier on him."

Jean handed him the sailor's card, then Mrs. Harrington and the girls left, carrying the woman's birds in their cages. Mrs. Harrington continued to worry about the remaining petrels and said she almost hoped Yansky would not come back so she could take the birds and care for them properly.

Louise dropped her off at her home, then the Danas continued to their own house. They were met at the door by Aunt Harriet, who had a cablegram in her hand. It was plain to see that she had been crying.

"Oh, I'm so glad you're back!" she exclaimed. "Read this!"

She held the piece of paper out for them to see. The message was short. It said:

CAPTAIN DANA SERIOUSLY ILL.
SHIP'S DOCTOR.

CHAPTER IX

Search for a Voice

THERE were tears in Aunt Harriet's eyes, but she said no more about her brother's condition. "I've phoned the steamship office repeatedly, but the line is always busy."

"Every relative of the passengers and crew on board the *Balaksa* is probably calling," Jean remarked. "We might never get through."

Louise put an arm around her aunt. "I have an idea. Why don't Jean and I go to New York City and visit the steamship company personally to see what we can find out about Uncle Ned?"

"That would be great!" Jean chimed in. "Aunt Harriet, please say yes!"

Miss Dana looked at her nieces fondly. "Your idea is good, but where would you stay? I don't want you all alone in a hotel!"

Louise had already thought of that. "I'm sure

we could visit Doris Harland. Her family has an apartment there."

Aunt Harriet managed to smile. "That would be fine."

Louise called Doris right away and the two friends chatted excitedly. They were on vacation from Starhurst School, which had had a flood and required extensive repairs. All the students had been sent home, and word had not yet come when they might return.

Doris was bubbling over. "Oh, visit me, by all means!" she said. "But why this sudden trip?"

Louise told her about the *Balaska*, the terrible hurricane, and the cablegram about Uncle Ned's illness.

"We're so worried about him that we've been trying to get the steamship company on the phone. The line is always busy. When Jean and I are in New York, we'll go there ourselves and find out more about our uncle."

Doris asked, "When will you come?"

"As soon as we can get a flight. We'll start packing right away. Oh, Doris, this will be marvellous. But listen, you haven't asked your parents whether it would be convenient for them. Please do that first."

"I will. Hold on a minute." Doris quickly found her mother, who came to the phone to talk to Louise.

"I'm dreadfully sorry about your uncle, dear," she said. "Of course we would welcome you here, and we are looking forward to seeing you."

Louise thanked Mrs. Harland and told Aunt Harriet that everything was settled. Jean called the airport and obtained reservations on a flight that would leave the next morning.

Then the girls hurried upstairs with their aunt to pack. "I don't think you'll need a lot of dresses," Aunt Harriet said. "You won't be there long."

Jean's eyes twinkled. "Aunt Harriet, you want this mystery solved as much as I do. And since Uncle Ned is involved in it, we might have to stay longer than you think. It may be cold or warm. We'd better take two types of clothing."

"You're right," Aunt Harriet admitted, and helped the girls choose sweaters, suits, dresses, and coats.

Louise declared she was going to wear good walking shoes. "And I'll pack a pair of high heeled ones in case I need them."

Cora came upstairs to clean. When she saw the suitcases, she looked at the girls in surprise. "You're not going off on a trip when we're in such trouble, are you?"

"No," Louise soothed her. "We're flying to New York to visit the steamship company to find out about Uncle Ned."

Cora was delighted to hear this. "You always

know just the right thing to do. Me, I seem to do everything wrong."

"Oh, Cora, you know that's not true," Jean said, and Louise added, "You must think positively, Cora, never negatively. Be a positive thinker. It really works."

"What's that?"

"If you want to accomplish a certain task, tell yourself that you'll be able to do it and that everything will turn out fine."

Cora sighed. "I suppose you're right. I always expect to do everything wrong, and that's why it mostly happens that way. But I'll try to change."

When it was time to leave, Aunt Harriet offered to drive the girls to the airport.

"Let's leave early," Jean suggested. "I'd like to stop at Mrs. Harrington's and tell her we're going to New York."

Mrs. Harrington thought the trip was a good idea. "I wish you luck," she added. "But remember what Cicero once said. 'Certain signs cometh before events.' So watch carefully."

Jean grinned. "We'll look around every corner before proceeding."

"Have you heard from the police about Emil Yansky?" Louise asked.

"They called me just a few minutes ago. Yansky did not return to the apartment, and they'll bring me his birds."

"I'm glad," Jean said.

Mrs. Harrington nodded. "The police questioned every tenant in his building," she went on. "None of them knew Yansky well. He kept to himself and never talked to anybody. Apparently he was out a great deal and rarely had visitors."

"A strange man," Jean remarked. "He must have been involved in some secret activity, but I doubt that he earned an honest living."

Mrs. Harrington and Louise agreed, then the girls said good-bye and left.

At the airport, Aunt Harriet had a few words of advice. "I want you to keep out of any difficult corners while in New York," she warned. Her nieces promised they would be careful, kissed her good-bye, and boarded the plane.

The flight was uneventful, and as soon as Louise and Jean arrived at their destination, they took a taxi to the steamship office. It was on a huge pier on the upper West side of the Hudson River waterfront. The receptionist recognized the girls and told them the president, Commodore Cooke, was in his office. She called him on the intercom and announced the visitors. He said he would be delighted to see them.

Louise and Jean went to his office. He was on the telephone and waved to them to sit down. His room had always fascinated the girls. The walls were covered with photographs of the steamship line's vessels, both passenger ships and freighters. Also displayed were pictures of the various captains. Louise and Jean gazed fondly at a portrait of Uncle Ned. What a fine-looking man he was! Tall and broad shouldered, he had a florid complexion, due to his life on the sea. His eyes twinkled merrily. Louise felt a sharp pain in her chest when she remembered that now Captain Dana lay desperately ill!

Commodore Cooke put down the telephone and greeted the sisters warmly. "I'm glad to see you. Are you in New York for a visit?"

The Danas were puzzled. They had expected him to be aware of why they had come. Immediately Louise began to talk about Uncle Ned. "We had a disturbing cablegram from the *Balaska* and wanted to find out more about it. We phoned and phoned you, but the line was always busy."

"We had a lot of calls because of the hurricane," the commodore confirmed.

"We're alarmed about our uncle," Jean took up the story. "We understand he's very ill. Besides, we were told that he's being blamed for the damage to the *Balaska* and the injuries to the passengers during the hurricane. We assume this means he might lose his position?"

The commodore's brow furrowed. "None of this is true!" he exclaimed. "Where did you hear this?"

"The cablegram was sent by the ship's doctor," Jean replied.

"I can't understand it," Commodore Cooke declared. "There must be a grave misunderstanding. Your uncle is fine. I talked to him just a little while ago. He's tired, of course, but okay."

Louise and Jean sighed in relief. "Then the cable was a fake," Jean said. "Could you track down the sender?"

"I'll try," the commodore answered. "But tell me, where did you get the information about charges against your uncle? That's not true, either!"

"From the man who answered your phone. The first time we called we were told that the number had been changed, and—"

"What! We haven't changed our number in thirty years!" Commodore Cooke exclaimed.

The Danas exchanged puzzled glances.

"I'm afraid this whole thing is a big hoax," the company president went on. "Your uncle is certainly not ill, and did a great bit of seamanship during the hurricane. If anything, he'll get a citation for excellent service!"

Louise sighed deeply. "I'm so glad. But I wonder who's playing this dreadful trick on us, and why!"

Jean asked the commodore if a second hurricane had followed the first one.

"Of course not. The whole thing is ridiculous. I'll make an investigation at once!"

Louise asked if she might use the telephone to call her aunt and relieve the poor woman's mind.

"Yes, indeed," Commodore Cooke said. "Go right ahead."

Miss Dana was delighted to hear the news. But she was as puzzled as the girls about the false information. "I wonder who told us the number had been changed," she said. "It must have been someone at the steamship office, who received my first call."

"Commodore Cooke is trying to find out," Louise said, then hung up.

The president asked Louise, "Could you identify the voice of the man to whom you spoke?"

Louise shook her head. "Only our Aunt Harriet talked to him," she replied.

"Well, I'll do my best to solve the mystery," Commodore Cooke promised.

Knowing that he was a busy man, the girls stood up to leave. "May we wander around your property and see if we can pick up a clue?" Jean asked.

The president smiled. "You do anything you like. The nearer you come to an answer to our problem, the more you help me."

The girls thanked him and said good-bye. When they reached the outer office, Jean told his secretary what had happened and asked if she had any idea who the culprit might be.

"I'm afraid not," the woman replied. "And I

can't believe someone told you our number had been changed!"

Louise and Jean went outside and walked around the dock, listening to various conversations between employees. Nothing pertained to their case. Finally they started toward the street. On the way they came to a fair-sized shack. Over the door was a sign: *Superintendent's Office.*

"Maybe he can tell us something," Jean suggested.

The girls knocked. No one answered, so they walked in. Louise approached the desk which stood in the middle of the room and stared at a notation on a pad. It was the Danas' name and address in Oak Falls!

"Jean, look at this!" she whispered excitedly.

Her sister peered over Louise's shoulder in wonder. Then her gaze fell on the telephone. "Louise!" she cried out. "The number on it is the one given to Aunt Harriet!"

"You mean that all this time she's been talking to the superintendent, and he gave her the wrong information?"

"It certainly seems that way."

"But why?" Louise asked.

Jean shrugged, then pointed to a scrap of paper lying on the desk. "And here's another Oak Falls number!" she exclaimed. "Let's write it down."

Louise took a pencil from the desk and wrote it

on a blank piece of paper, while Jean looked around the room. On a nearby table she spotted a second telephone. On it was the steamship line's number!

"Now I know what happened," she declared. "Aunt Harriet's first call, for some reason, was intercepted by the superintendent. When he learned who she was, he told her the number had been changed. Then she called back on the other line, and he fed her the false information!"

Her sister set her jaw. "You're right. We'd better find that man in a hurry!"

CHAPTER X

Revealing Phone Call

JEAN put a restraining hand on her sister's shoulder. "We'd better be cautious," she warned. "We don't want to accuse the wrong man. It's possible someone else has been using this shack!"

"All right," Louise said. "You have a point. But let me make a phone call." She picked up the instrument on the table and dialled the operator.

"May I help you?" a woman answered.

"Yes," Louise replied. "I'm in the superintendent's office, but he's not here. Have you any idea where he might be?"

"He must be on the dock somewhere," the operator replied. "He was in the hospital, but he's been back to work since the beginning of the week."

"Does he have an assistant?"

"No. Would you like to speak to anyone else?"

"No, thank you," Louise said and hung up. She repeated the conversation to Jean.

"What next?" her sister asked.

On a hunch Louise picked up the other phone. There was no dial tone. The instrument was dead! She followed the cord to the wall and discovered that the phone was unplugged. "Funny he's using a jack instead of having the phone permanently installed," she commented.

The girls left the shack, intending to go back to the president's office. A man passed them on the way. Jean watched him and realized he was going to the superintendent's building.

She grabbed Louise by the sleeve. "Come on, let's follow him."

The man went inside, but did not close the door. The Danas tiptoed up to it and stood listening. They heard him dialling a number, then he said, "Tredway here. We need more two-by-fours." He hung up seconds later. The girls did not want to be caught spying, so they hurried off.

On the way to Commodore Cooke's office, Jean said, "I wish Aunt Harriet were here. She might be able to identify Tredway as the man she spoke to."

"If we don't make any progress on the case, perhaps we should ask her to come to New York," Louise suggested.

"Good idea," Jean agreed. "But first let's talk it over with the president. After all, he's in charge here and should know what's going on."

"We should also call the Oak Falls Police and have them trace the number we found," Louise said.

Commodore Cooke was free to talk to the girls, and when they walked in, he smiled. "I didn't expect to see you back so soon. Don't tell me you've solved the mystery!"

"No, but we may have picked up worthwhile information," Louise replied. "Is your superintendent's name Tredway?"

"Yes, it is."

The girls told him what they had seen and heard during the last half hour.

Commodore Cooke was amazed, especially about the second telephone in Tredway's office. He had no explanation why the superintendent had ordered more two-by-fours, but felt they were needed for one of the ships. "I'll check on the telephones," he promised the girls, "and will let you know what I find out. Where will you be?"

Louise gave him the Harlands' address and telephone number. Then she asked if she and Jean might call the Oak Falls Police Department.

"Sure. Go ahead. I'm curious myself to know whose number that was in Tredway's office."

Jean talked to Captain Murphy. "I'll be glad to

find out for you," he said. "Where are you now?"

Upon learning they were in New York City, he said, "Tell me where you can be reached, and I'll call you back in a few minutes." Louise did so.

While they were waiting, the girls talked to Commodore Cooke. Finally Captain Murphy in Oak Falls phoned and said that the number they had found was unlisted.

"The subscriber is Randy Mercek!" the captain added.

Louise and Jean looked at each other. What a wonderful clue!

Commodore Cooke smiled. "Did Captain Murphy have interesting news?"

"Yes, he did," Louise replied. "We know the man whose number we found, and we hope that this will help us solve the mystery."

"You're very smart detectives," Commodore Cooke said. "I'm sure you'll figure out the answer to the puzzle."

The girls stood up and said good-bye for the second time that day. "And now we really mean it," Jean added with a grin.

He laughed. "I haven't had such interesting visitors in a long time. You come again. Meanwhile, I'll investigate our superintendent."

Louise and Jean set off in a taxi to the Harlands' apartment house. They went in, took a lift up, and rang the bell.

The door flew open and Doris, a pretty, blue-eyed blonde, clasped both Danas in her arms. "Oh, this is simply super!" she exclaimed. "Come on in. Mother and Dad have been as eager to see you as I have."

The Danas greeted Doris's parents. Her father, a lawyer, said, "How are you enjoying your enforced vacation?"

Louise replied, "So far it's been very exciting."

The group sat down to talk. The Harlands were interested in hearing the details of the mystery, and when Louise mentioned the name Emil Yansky, Mr. Harland held up a hand. "Wait a minute!"

The Danas looked at him in surprise as he went on, "You know, I have a lot of maritime clients. That name rings a bell. Let me make a couple of phone calls to refresh my memory."

He went into his study. Meanwhile, the three girls talked about their friends at Starhurst School. Doris had heard from Evelyn Starr and Ann Freeman. The group was still giggling and exchanging stories when Mr. Harland returned.

"I have some real news for you Danas," he said. "Emil Yansky was in trouble with the law in connection with a gang of sailors who were thieves."

Jean and Louise caught their breaths. So the witch was a hardened criminal!

"What was the outcome of the case?" Louise asked. "Did Yansky go to prison?"

"No," Mr. Harland replied. "He claimed he had

nothing to do with the thefts and only acted as lookout. He was given a fine, which he paid. After that, he disappeared and apparently had nothing more to do with the sea and ships, since he's not registered anywhere now."

"I wonder if he tries to have people think he's making a living by raising petrels," Doris said.

The others laughed.

Some time later Commodore Cooke called the Danas. He reported that Superintendent Tredway, who had a clean record, had denied all accusations. He had put a private phone in his shack to use when the company's switchboard was not in operation.

Louise and Jean were sure this was not the only reason. Louise asked, "Did he list the second number in the name of the steamship company?"

"No," the president replied. "It's unlisted."

"Can you get a copy of his bills to find out what numbers he called?"

Commodore Cooke said he would need an order from the police to obtain that information. "If no satisfactory clues to your mystery turn up in the next few days, I'll get one. Please let me know how you progress."

"Do you suppose someone else could be using Tredway's private phone when he isn't in the shack?" Doris spoke up after Louise had finished the call.

"It's possible," Louise conceded. "We could have. His office door was unlocked, and we walked right in."

A short time later there was another call for the Danas. It came from Aunt Harriet. She had received a telegram from Uncle Ned, confirming that the *Balaska* was definitely going to dock the next morning.

"Be sure you go down and meet him," she said. "Then let me know how he really is."

"What time will the ship come in?" Louise asked.

Miss Dana said it was supposed to arrive about eight o'clock, and that passengers would be disembarking by nine.

Louise and Jean were so excited at the news that they did not sleep very well that night. They kept waking, wondering whether it was time to get up yet. They wanted to be at the pier the instant the *Balaska* came into sight.

Doris asked to come along, and the Danas were glad to have her. "Uncle Ned will be surprised to see you," Jean said. "And he'll be happy to know that we're staying with your family."

After an early breakfast, the three girls set off in a cab. When they reached the pier, it was bustling with activity, and they had a hard time making their way through the crowd. Relatives and friends of the passengers had heard that the vessel had been in a hurricane and were eager to meet their loved ones.

Sharply at nine o'clock people began to disembark. Most of them looked all right, but now and then someone would hobble off on crutches or have a bandaged arm.

Louise inquired about going aboard and was told that no one was allowed to enter the ship until all passengers had left. This meant a long wait, and the three became fidgety.

Finally, however, an official standing at the foot of the gangplank waved for them to go ahead. "Watch your step," he warned. "The ship's tossing a bit."

Jean ran up first and hurried across the deck toward a stairway that led to Uncle Ned's quarters. She had not reached it yet when suddenly a door opened and a man dashed out. He wore a raincoat with the collar turned up, and a felt hat was pulled low over his face.

Jean paid no attention to him. He followed her silently and suddenly lifted her up. Before she could struggle out of his arms, he tossed her overboard!

CHAPTER XI

Kidnap Attempt

Louise and Doris, who were close on Jean's heels, heard her scream. In a flash Louise decided what to do. Knowing her sister was a good swimmer, she ran after the attacker.

"Doris, watch Jean!" she called back over her shoulder. "I'll try to catch that man!"

Doris ran to the railing and looked down. Jean had just missed hitting a motorboat with two men in it. They offered to help her climb in, but she refused. Was she suspicious of them?

With powerful strokes the girl swam to the ship's ladder. To Doris's surprise, the men pulled their boat alongside and tried to reach her, but she scooted up the rungs so quickly that they did not succeed.

Halfway up the ladder, Jean paused and called

down to the men. "Who are you? What do you want from me?"

"Just keep out of our affairs!" one of them answered.

Doris's long friendship with the Danas had taught her to react fast. From her handbag she took a small, instant camera that she had brought with her, intending to photograph the *Balaska*. Quickly she snapped a series of pictures of the men and their boat. She even caught the name painted on its side, *The Petrel*, before the craft chugged off.

Doris smiled. Then she separated the negatives from the pictures, discarded the former, and put the photographs in her pocketbook.

Looking for Jean, she went toward the ship's ladder. The young detective had arrived on the deck, dripping wet and out of breath. Doris looked at her dishevelled appearance and could not help but laugh. "You're a mess. We'd better take you somewhere and clean you up!"

Jean nodded. "We'll go to Uncle Ned's quarters. Did you get any pictures? I saw you with the camera."

"Yes, I did. I also noticed that the boat was called *The Petrel.*"

"So did I. That's why I didn't get in. I'm sure the men are part of the gang we're dealing with. Where's Louise?"

"I don't know. She took off after your attacker," Doris replied.

"What did the man look like?" Jean inquired. "I couldn't tell because he sneaked up behind me."

"He was short and heavyset. He wore a hat pulled low, but a strand of dark hair fell down his forehead."

At once Jean realized that the description fitted Randy Mercek. On the way to Captain Dana's quarters, she told Doris about her suspicion.

"I think you're right," her friend agreed. "Well, here we are."

Before Jean could knock, the door flew open and Captain Dana gave her a big hug. Then he said hello to Doris. His face was serious and he appeared upset.

"Aren't you surprised about the way I look?" Jean asked.

"I heard what happened a minute ago. One of my crew members was down at the pier and saw you being thrown overboard. He didn't recognize the man who did it, however. I was just on my way out to look for you. Where's Louise?"

"She followed Jean's attacker," Doris explained. "She really should be back by now."

"I haven't seen her yet," Captain Dana said, then frowned. "Jean, do you have any idea who your attacker was?"

"Yes. A man named Randy Mercek. He's in with a gang, I believe, and his companions tried to pick me up in a boat named *The Petrel*."

"I'll bet you're working on another mystery!" the captain exclaimed.

"We are, and it involves you and the *Balaska!*" Jean replied.

"You must tell me all about it!"

"May I take off these soggy clothes first? Then I'll give you the details."

"By all means," Uncle Ned said. "You'll find an outfit in my bathroom that belongs to one of my assistants. He's very slight, and I think it'll fit you."

"Just pretend you're a sailor until your clothes are dry," Doris added with a chuckle.

"At this point I'm too cold to be choosy," Jean declared. "I'll wear anything!" She disappeared into the bathroom.

"Doris, have a seat," Uncle Ned said. "I want to call the harbour police and tell them about the incident so they can look out for that boat. Can you describe it for me?"

"Sure," Doris said. "Even better, I can show you a picture of it." She explained how she had been able to photograph the men and their craft and pulled out the evidence.

"Terrific!" Uncle Ned praised her. "This will

make it easier to find the culprits." He went to the telephone and gave the Harbour Police a detailed description of the fugitives. After a brief conversation, he hung up.

"While Jean is changing her clothes, I'd like to go and find Louise," Doris said.

"Okay. I'll wait for Jean, then we'll join you," Captain Dana replied.

Doris left his quarters and went down to the deck below. She walked around and asked several sailors if they had seen Louise, but no one had.

After Louise had watched the stranger throw her sister overboard, she saw him run up a flight of stairs. The girl dashed after him. She caught a glimpse of him as he turned into a corridor at the top, and she followed.

The chase led down another stairway to the deck. When Louise had almost reached him, the suspect grabbed a deck chair and flung it in her way, hoping she would fall and be delayed in her effort.

Instead, the girl leaped over it nimbly and resumed her pursuit. She was surprised how well he seemed to know the ship. Had he been a passenger or a member of the crew at some time?

The case led through a door and down another stairway. By the time Louise reached the bottom, the fugitive was nowhere to be seen. The young detective was stumped. Had he taken a cross corridor or disappeared into a cabin? She stood still, wondering which way to go.

Just then she heard a lift door slam. Quickly she turned the corner to the spot where several lifts were located. A light on one indicated that it was descending. Louise rang for the lift next to it. The door opened, and she dashed inside. She pushed a button to take her down. Just then she heard a rustling noise behind her.

Louise turned and froze in terror! Randy Mercek was crouched in one corner. With an evil grin, he rose and approached her. She tried to reach the alarm button, but Mercek pushed her aside.

"I'm in charge now, you little busybody!" he snarled.

Louise screamed as she watched the angry man pull a handkerchief from his pocket. He pinned her arms behind her back and held them in place with one strong hand. With the other, he stuffed the gag into her mouth as she shrieked for help.

Louise struggled fiercely, and for a moment she got one hand loose to push the emergency button. Instantly Mercek grabbed her again. The lift had descended two decks, but it did not stop. Apparently he had managed to turn off the alarm button and had programmed the elevator to take them all the way down.

"You Danas learn your lessons the hard way!" he hissed and held Louise even tighter. She was trying to get the wad of cloth out of her mouth and finally succeeded.

"What do you mean?" she sputtered. "And what are you going to do with me?"

"You'll see!" Mercek grinned evilly and pulled a second handkerchief from his pocket. As Louise screamed for help, he pushed it between her teeth. "I'm going to put you where you can't do any more spying!" he declared.

CHAPTER XII

Eavesdropper!

THE lift in which Louise was being held a prisoner finally stopped. The door opened and Randy Mercek pushed her out, still holding her arms behind her back. Louise recognized the location as part of the crew's quarters.

She tried to scream, but this time the gag was tight, and no sound escaped her throat. Mercek yanked her toward a storage room, opened it, and shoved her in. Then he quickly locked the door.

It was pitch black inside the room, and Louise stood still. Now that her hands were free, she could pull the gag from her mouth. What a relief! Then she pounded on the door and yelled for help over and over again. Nothing happened. Finally Louise gave up.

The nearly exhausted girl sat down on the floor

and tried to figure out how she could escape. With most of the crew on shore leave, her shouting might not be heard until the next day!

She decided there must be a light in the storage room and felt around near the door. Finally her fingers touched a small switch. She clicked it on and breathed a sigh of relief.

A dim light flooded the small room, and she could look around. Her eyes came to rest on a telephone on the wall. Would it work?

Tensely she picked up the instrument and listened. There was neither a dial tone nor a response on the other end. Apparently the operator was not on duty.

"Now what'll I do?" Louise asked herself desperately. She put the phone back on the hook and stood still, determined to figure out something.

Suddenly an idea came to her. "I remember Uncle Ned's number in his quarters. Hopefully it hasn't changed!" She picked up the receiver again and dialled the number with trembling fingers. Nothing happened.

Louise bit her lips, and tears welled up in her eyes. She was about to hang up when she heard a click. "Captain Dana!" a familiar voice boomed.

"Oh, Uncle Ned, it's Louise!" the girl cried out. "I'm locked in a storage room in the crew's quarters on the bottom deck. Please come and let me out."

"I'm so glad it's you!" Uncle Ned replied. "We

were just about to go out and look for you. We'll be down in a minute."

The captain did not waste any time asking Louise how she had gotten into the storage room. Instead, he, Jean, and Doris went to the bottom deck as fast as they could.

With a master key he unlocked the door of his niece's prison and hugged her in joy and relief. Now that the tense moments were over, the girl burst into laughter when she noticed Jean's costume.

"Hi, sailor," she said. "How did you like your bath in the river?"

"Not much," her sister replied. "I'll tell you all about it when we get upstairs."

The group returned to Uncle Ned's quarters and settled in comfortable chairs. He poured everyone a glass of fresh apple cider, then stories were exchanged.

When Louise told about how she had been kidnapped, Doris became furious. "How dreadful!" she cried out. "I hope we'll catch this mean man so he can go to jail!"

Uncle Ned agreed, but nevertheless, looked at his nieces proudly. "I certainly must congratulate you on your fortitude!" he said. "Just the same, I'm sorry you've been put through such an experience, and I mean to get to the bottom of this mystery!"

"How are you going to do that?" Doris asked.

Captain Dana said that first he would call the dock security guards and quiz them about people getting on and off the ship. In a little while, two men appeared.

Uncle Ned showed them the photographs Doris had taken and questioned them about *The Petrel* and Jean's attacker. They had not seen anyone leaving the ship in the last twenty minutes, and before that, only crew members and passengers had come ashore.

Jean spoke up. "Do you suppose Mercek is still hiding on the *Balaska?*"

"Unless he's getting off while we're up here," one of the guards replied.

"My guess is that he would have wanted to leave as soon as possible," Captain Dana said. "Perhaps he got away in a boat."

"*The Petrel?*" Louise asked.

"I think it would have been too dangerous for *The Petrel* to return. But his mates could have picked him up in another craft."

"I think we should search the ship in case he's still aboard," Louise suggested.

"I agree," Captain Dana said. He told the security men to go back to their posts and said he would call the sailors who were still on duty to help with the search.

Before the guards left, one of them said, "Something happened at the pier when the passengers disembarked. I don't know if it has something to do with your case—"

"What is it?" the captain inquired.

"While people were waiting at various locations to have their baggage examined by the customs officials for undeclared articles, a man came up to me and offered me a bribe."

"What!" Captain Dana burst out.

"He wanted me to let his bags go through without being inspected. I don't know what he had that he didn't want the officials to see and if it has anything to do with your mystery."

"It could," Jean declared. "Who was this person?"

"A man named Roy Stryker. His address was care of Uptown Gems, New York City."

"I wonder if that's his right name and business address," Louise remarked.

"I don't know," the guard replied. "And I can't tell you anything else."

"Thank you," Captain Dana said, and the two men left.

"Unless Stryker had a phony passport, I think it must have been his real name," Uncle Ned said, "because all passports were examined. But we'd better look this man up as soon as we go ashore."

The others agreed, then Captain Dana called a number of men to help in the hunt for Mercek.

He asked some officers to watch all exits, then led the rest of the crew to the sailors' quarters to begin their search.

They checked the rooms in groups of two or three. The girls stayed with Uncle Ned and investigated cabin after cabin without results. Finally they came to a room Uncle Ned said was occupied by a seaman named Hal Humpmeyer. He was not there. Jean noticed a letter on his dresser. The sender was Emil Yansky!

"A message from the witch!" she cried out and held the letter up for all to see.

Captain Dana gazed at it for several seconds, then said, "Under the circumstances, I, as captain of this ship, have the right to open this letter and read it. We know Yansky is in league with Mercek, and Mercek is guilty of assault and attempted kidnapping!"

The girls watched intently as he took out a sheet of paper, first reading it to himself.

"Can't we hear the contents?" Louise asked.

Her uncle nodded. "This is very damaging evidence, not only against Yansky, but against Hal Humpmeyer as well. It reveals that Yansky worked on the *Balaska* once under an assumed name. He and Hal have been friends for a long time."

"What else does it say?" Jean urged impatiently.

"Besides references to their friendship and Yansky's stint on the *Balaska*, there's only one more sentence," Uncle Ned replied. "It says, 'The goods were safely delivered, thanks to you!' "

The girls looked at each other, then Doris exclaimed, "Smugglers!"

"I'm afraid so," Captain Dana agreed.

His nieces were shocked, and Jean remarked, "Smugglers working on this ship! How dreadful!"

"And I thought the security on board was excellent," Uncle Ned said. He, too, was shocked to hear that underhanded business had been carried on.

Louise said, "I believe this is the answer to why we Danas have been harassed. First the petrel gang tried to intimidate us, then they attempted to scare us with those false reports about Uncle Ned's problems with the *Balaska*. They must have thought you were suspicious and wanted to get you off the ship, Uncle Ned!"

Doris spoke up. "And the fact that Louise and Jean are detectives must have caused the gang to be afraid. That's why they bothered them so often."

Uncle Ned nodded. "How many people seem to be involved in this gang so far?"

The count included Emil Yansky, Mercek, Humpmeyer, Tredway, and perhaps Roy Stryker of Uptown Gems.

"Maybe a further search of the ship will yield

even more suspects," Uncle Ned said. "Let's continue."

They canvassed the rest of the sailors' cabins, then met with the other crew members in Uncle Ned's quarters to compare notes. No further evidence had turned up.

Uncle Ned thanked the officers and seamen who had helped, then dismissed them. The Danas and Doris remained to analyse what they had learned.

"If we turn the matter over to the police, they still do not have enough proof to make any arrests," Uncle Ned said. "Yet it seems like a big order to keep all these gang members under surveillance. I wonder if I shouldn't ask a good detective agency to help us."

Louise and Jean stared at him in dismay. "Oh, please, not yet!" Jean said. "Don't you think Louise and I have made a good start on solving the mystery?"

Her uncle admitted that, indeed, they had. He smiled. "Well, I'll give you a little longer, but you'll have to promise me that you won't let yourselves run into unnecessary danger. Be very careful where you go and to whom you speak. I don't want any more abductions or attempts to harm you!"

As the Danas assured him they would use great caution, Doris suddenly got up from her chair. She tiptoed across the cabin, putting a finger to her lips to keep the others from commenting. Then she quickly yanked the door open.

A man tumbled inside from a crouching, listening position!

CHAPTER XIII

Suspicious Seamen

THE embarrassed eavesdropper proved to be a crew member. He stood up and apologized profusely.

"I didn't do anything wrong," he insisted. "Captain, you remember me, don't you? I'm Fred Bowsky."

"Yes. But what were you doing in front of my door?"

"I was listening to see if you had company. I wanted to ask a favour of you but didn't mean to disturb you if you had guests."

The excuse sounded plausible. Uncle Ned said, "What did you want to ask me?"

"Well, I'm not off duty tonight. But I'd like a short shore leave to do an errand. It's very important," Fred Bowsky replied.

Captain Dana did not grant permission right away. Instead, he said, "Do you know a passenger named Roy Stryker?"

"A little," Fred answered. "I'm in charge of deck chairs, and he got one from me every day. Is there anything you wanted to ask me about Mr. Stryker?"

Uncle Ned was cagey. "I didn't get to speak to him, and I wondered what he was like."

"Oh, he was a nice guy," Fred replied. "But I really didn't know him that well—just fixing his chair and blanket for him every day."

Captain Dana asked how long Bowsky wished to remain on shore.

The crewman answered immediately, "Just a short time. A couple of hours."

"All right, you may leave for two hours. When you return, report to me." The captain sat down at his desk and wrote out a permission slip for the man. "Remember," he repeated, "you're to report to me when you come back."

Fred Bowsky bowed slightly. "Yes, sir. Thank you, sir."

After he had left, Doris spoke up. "Captain Dana, my parents would like to invite you to dinner tonight. Would that be possible?"

Uncle Ned sighed. "I wish I could accept. But with all that's happened on board the *Balaska* recently, I'd better stay here in case I'm needed."

Doris was disappointed. "I'm sorry," she said. "Mom and Dad were really looking forward to meeting you."

Captain Dana patted her on the shoulder. "I'll tell you what we can do. Suppose your parents come here, and we'll all have dinner on board ship?"

"That would be great!" Doris said gleefully. She looked at Louise and Jean. "Okay with you?"

"Fine," the sisters replied.

Doris phoned her family, and they gladly accepted the invitation. They promised to be on the ship at seven o'clock.

Captain Dana called the chef on duty and gave him the necessary instructions. When the girls overheard the menu, they knew it would be a delicious meal.

Starting with shrimp cocktail, it was to include steak, mashed potatoes, fresh broccoli with hollandaise sauce, and a mixed green salad with tomato and cucumber. For dessert there would be apple pie topped with vanilla ice cream.

Doris laughed. "Captain Dana, I think your guests will burst!"

Uncle Ned chuckled, then Louise asked him if she could use his telephone to bring Aunt Harriet up to date on what had happened.

"Go right ahead," he replied. "I'm not expecting any business calls."

Aunt Harriet was surprised to hear about the new developments in the case. "You seem to be getting into all kinds of trouble," she said worriedly, then told Louise that the police had called her. "A detective saw Emil Yansky in a car in the centre of town. Unfortunately, it went by so quickly that the officer didn't get the licence number. It proves, however, that Yansky's still in Oak Falls, even though he hasn't returned to his home."

"I'm glad we rescued those birds," Louise said. "The poor things would have starved to death."

Aunt Harriet agreed. "Mrs. Harrington wants you to know that all the petrels are getting along just fine," she added. "I was over there this morning, and they were chirping happily as if to tell their new mistress how content they were."

When Mr. and Mrs. Harland arrived in the evening, they were amazed to hear about the day's events and were talking about the mystery on the way to the captain's private dining room. Their host cautioned them not to mention the case in front of the waiter, however.

"I don't know him very well," Captain Dana said, "and at this point I think we should be very careful."

The waiter, whose name was Wells, turned out to be quite talkative. He asked questions about the visitors and added, "Aren't you folks going out on the town later on?"

Mr. Harland smiled. "We hadn't planned to."

"Oh, but you're missing all the fun of the big city!" Wells told them. "It would be a shame not to enjoy some of the amusements."

The more he talked, the more Doris became convinced that she should entertain her guests. Finally she said, "I think seeing New York at night would be a good idea. Let's go out!"

The Danas hesitated. The waiter had been so insistent that it appeared as if he wanted them to leave the ship for a reason. Did he have any ulterior motive?

But Doris would not take no for an answer. After Wells had left the room, Jean said, "I have an idea. Perhaps we can take your father's car and go to places the sailors frequent. We might pick up a clue about one of our suspects."

Doris was disappointed that Jean had not suggested the theatre or a concert, but she did not show it. "That's fine with me," she said.

Mr. Harland added, "I'll go with you. It might not be safe for you girls to walk around these places by yourselves."

A few minutes later the waiter cleared the table and left. Louise, who had not overcome her suspicion of him, said, "I still believe that man was trying to get rid of us. I'd like to stay and do some sleuthing on board. Suppose I go to the gangplank with you, so it appears as if all of us are leaving, and then I'll double back. You don't mind, do you?"

Jean chuckled. "Of course not. We can have a race and see which of us discovers the most clues!"

"Agreed!"

Uncle Ned looked at Louise. "Remember, if you need help, I'll be here."

"I think I'll go back to the apartment instead of coming with you girls," Mrs. Harland announced. "I'm a bit tired and don't quite feel up to a night out. I'll take a taxi."

Captain Dana phoned for a cab, then turned to Louise. "Please do your sleuthing out-of-doors," he requested. "A good part of the ship is dark, and I don't want anything to happen to you."

"I will," the girl promised, then the group left. Chatting loudly, they made their way to the gangplank, hoping the waiter would realize that they were going. Just before they left the ship, Louise stepped into a narrow corridor.

All was quiet. She stood close to the wall and listened, but nothing happened. After five minutes, she doubled back to the deck. Keeping close to the side, she wandered from one end to the other. The ship seemed to be deserted.

Suddenly, as Louise neared the stern, she heard

a strange noise. She stepped forward and looked over the railing but could see nothing. Quickly she scooted down an iron stairway to the deck below. From here she had a good view of the pier. A gangplank was set up at the rear of the ship. A small keg was rolling down to the dock, where it was caught by a seaman. Then another one was sent, and another.

Louise was puzzled. Why were they unloading cargo at such a late hour? She remembered having seen similar kegs in France during a visit there. They contained sacramental wine and had been delivered to a church.

"If that's what's in those barrels, why are the men so secretive about it?" Louise thought. She strained her eyes to see if there was any printing on the containers that might identify their destination and the sender. However, from where she stood, it was impossible to detect anything in the dim light.

Forgetting that she was to be cautious, Louise went to the open hatch. A keg rolled near her. She leaned across the gangplank to get a closer look. Just then another barrel came along. It hit her hard, knocking her down!

The keg veered off course through the impact and rolled into the water! As Louise arose, a seaman rushed up to her. She noticed the name on his overalls.

Hal Humpmeyer!

His face was red with anger. "What are you doing here?" he shouted. "You were supposed to have gone ashore! I ought to throw you into the water for punishment!"

CHAPTER XIV

Finders' Keepers

The keg that had hit Louise was drifting away from the stern of the ocean liner. A passing motorboat approached it, and one of the two men in it reached out with both hands to scoop it up.

When Hal Humpmeyer saw him, he shouted down, "Hey! Bring that back!"

The man merely laughed.

"It doesn't belong to you!" Humpmeyer yelled. "It fell off this ship!"

"Forget it!" the stranger called out. "Finders' keepers, finders' keepers!"

The seaman who had caught the kegs at the dock was furious. "You're thieves! Give us that barrel or we'll call the police!"

The men in the motorboat paid no attention. Still laughing, they roared away into the darkness.

Louise, who had been the cause of the accident, was frightened. She did not want to become involved with these coarse men. Hal Humpmeyer paid no attention to her, still calling and gesticulating after the men in the disappearing motorboat.

Quickly the girl scooted through the open hatch and hid behind a pile of boxes.

The sailor who had caught the kegs below, came up the gangplank. "Where's that girl?" he asked Humpmeyer.

Hal looked around. "Apparently she got scared and ran off."

"Who is she?"

"I think she's related to the captain, and I don't like the idea of her spying on us," Humpmeyer grumbled.

The other man shrugged. "Oh, well, she's gone now."

"And so is the keg. How are we going to explain this to our customer when they're delivered?"

"We'll just have to lie about it and say there was a shortage."

"You're right," Humpmeyer agreed. "We'll forget it." He broke out into a laugh. "I'll bet that guy who stole the keg will enjoy that sacramental wine!"

Louise was sure by now that the kegs contained something else besides the wine. But perhaps it was so well hidden that the men in the motorboat would never discover the contraband. In this way they would not go to the police, and the crooked crew members would not be accused of doing anything illegal, like smuggling. And even if the men found the undeclared goods, would they report it to the authorities?

As Louise's eyes became accustomed to the dimness of the hold, she noticed that one of the kegs stood not far from her. Hoping she would not be seen, the young sleuth tiptoed over to read the label. It bore the name *James Pruden, Incorporated, New York City*. What was even more interesting was a symbol painted below the address—a likeness of a storm petrel!

"These men are mixed up with the petrel gang!" Louise thought.

She decided to report the incident to Captain Dana at once. Maybe she would be in time to stop the shipment and call in the police!

Just then she heard a car pull up on the dock. Quickly the men descended the gangplank. When their steps had faded, Louise emerged from her hiding place and looked down. A keg was loaded into the trunk of the car!

Louise waited no longer. She ran up several stairways until she reached Uncle Ned's quarters, and burst in. No one was there.

"Oh, dear, what shall I do?" she asked herself.

Finally she decided that since there was no proof

of any wrongdoing, she should not call the police. It was better to wait for Uncle Ned to return. She would let him handle the whole matter.

Jean, Doris, and Mr. Harland, meanwhile, had driven to the area that the lawyer knew sailors frequented. The streets were narrow and full of people, many of them from the ships. There were several discotheques, with loud music blaring from them.

"Would you like to stop and look into one of the discos?" Mr. Harland asked.

"Yes," Jean replied. "Let's try the one we just passed. It seems larger and a little more fancy than the others."

Doris's father parked the car, and the trio walked up to the door. Two sailors lounged outside, leaning against the wall. When they saw the girls, they perked up.

"Hello, sweetheart!" one of them said to Jean.

She paid no attention.

Another sailor smirked at Doris. "Hey, you're pretty. I'd like to date you!"

Doris ignored him. The sailors laughed, and the younger one, a short fellow with curly dark hair, said, "We're not bad guys. We just want to take you girls inside and dance with you. How about it?"

Jean spoke up. "Thank you, but we already have an escort."

The young man looked at Mr. Harland. "You mean this old guy?" He shrugged. "Well, I suppose he has a lot more money than we do."

Jean did not comment, but asked instead, "Do you know Hal Humpmeyer?"

"No."

"Emil Yansky?"

The two seamen looked at each other. Finally the older one asked, "You mean that goon who worships storm petrels?"

"That's the one."

"Listen, girlie, take my advice and stay away from that guy. Don't mess around with him. He's a double-crosser."

Mr. Harland asked, "Is he in the disco?"

"I reckon he is. Whenever Yansky's in New York, he always hangs out in this place."

The two sailors started for the door. Jean called after them, "If you see Emil Yansky in there, tell him we want to talk to him."

"We'll do that," the curly-haired man promised.

At that moment two policemen in a squad car pulled up at the curb but did not get out. Apparently they were just on a routine check of the area.

Jean walked over to speak to them. "Would you please wait here a little while?" she asked. "I may need your help."

"What's your problem?" the driver asked.

At this moment, the young, curly-haired sailor emerged from the disco.

"This man has a message for me," Jean said to the officer. "Excuse me a moment, but please don't drive away."

She joined the others, and the seaman reported that Emil Yansky was indeed in the disco. He wanted to know who was asking for him.

"Shall I go in again and tell him?" the sailor inquired.

"Thank you, but I'll tell him myself," Jean replied.

First, she went back to the squad car and explained to the officers that a thief, whom she had been trying to track down, was in the disco. "Would one of you please come with me?" she asked.

The officer on the passenger side stepped out. Before acceding to Jean's request, he spoke to Mr. Harland to confirm the girl's story.

"All right," he said finally. "Let's go in."

He and Jean walked through the door, followed by the sailor. "What's going on, anyway?" the young seaman asked, puzzled.

Jean avoided a direct answer. "Yansky was in the town where I live. I just want to talk to him."

After threading their way between dancing couples and spectators, the trio reached the spot where Emil Yansky had been. The curly-haired seaman stared in surprise. "He's gone!" he exclaimed. "I'm sorry, miss."

Jean and the officer asked several people if they knew where Yansky was. Finally a young girl said, "I saw him a few minutes ago. He walked out of the fire door."

Jean thanked the sailor for his trouble, then she and the officer went out to Doris and Mr. Harland.

"What happened?" Doris asked eagerly.

"Unfortunately, Emil Yansky got away through the fire door," Jean replied.

The policeman spoke up. "If you don't need me any longer, I'll go back to my post."

Mr. Harland thanked the officer and said, "If you come across Emil Yansky, please hold him until you get in touch with me." He pulled a business card from his pocket and handed it to the policeman.

"We'll do that," the officer promised, then joined his colleague. The two men drove away.

Mr. Harland turned to Jean. "What do you want to do now?"

Jean admitted that she did not know. "Why don't we just drive up one block and down another? Maybe we'll pick up a clue to Emil Yansky."

Doris's father agreed, and they climbed into his car. He started off, and for ten minutes they cruised around the area. But there was no sign of

Emil Yansky. The group was about to give up their sleuthing and go back to the ship when Jean spotted the thief.

"He's going down into that underground station!" she cried out. "Let's follow him!"

Quickly Mr. Harland parked the car. The three ran to the underground entrance and dashed down the stairs after the fugitive!

CHAPTER XV

Mysterious Messages

As Yansky's pursuers reached the bottom of the stairs, the doors were just closing on a train. The fugitive stood inside, grinning at them maliciously. Then the train pulled out of the station.

Jean, Doris, and Mr. Harland had lost their quarry!

"We almost had that thief in our hands, and now he's gone!" Jean said angrily.

"Well, there's nothing we can do," Mr. Harland remarked. "Why don't we return to the ship and see if there is any news on the case."

The girls agreed. It was almost eleven o'clock when the group reached the *Balaska*. The crew members who had had shore leave were straggling back, two or three at a time.

Mr. Harland asked Jean about curfew hour. She did not know, so he inquired when they arrived at Captain Dana's quarters.

"Tonight it's eleven o'clock," the captain replied. "By the way, Fred Bowsky has not reported back yet."

Ten minutes after eleven, Captain Dana checked on the crew by telephone. All the men had returned, except Bowsky and Humpmeyer!

"Do you suppose they're in league with each other?" Jean spoke up.

"I don't know what to think," Captain Dana answered. "I really have a problem with my men overstaying their leave. I'll give them a little longer."

Doris wanted to know what had happened while they were gone, and Louise told her story. The others were amazed to hear about the kegs she had seen.

"Unfortunately, by the time Uncle Ned came back and I told him about it, the two men and the car into which they had loaded the barrels were gone," Louise ended her report.

"What about the keg in the hold with the name Pruden on it?" Jean inquired.

"That's gone, too," her sister replied. Then she turned to her uncle. "Would you like us to investigate the Pruden Company tomorrow morning?" she asked.

"That would be a good idea. Perhaps you could also check with Uptown Gems on Roy Stryker."

The girls nodded, then Mr. Harland suggested that they return to the apartment. They said good night to Captain Dana and walked down the gangplank. A guard smiled at them.

"Did Bowsky and Humpmeyer ever come aboard?" Mr. Harland inquired.

"No, sir, they didn't."

"We shouldn't have trusted Bowsky," Jean said when they were out of earshot of the guard. "Now we know he eavesdropped on purpose!"

"Of course," Louise said. "But he seemed like a nice guy, and his request for a short leave appeared honest."

"Honest! I'm sure he's mixed up with the petrel gang."

The following morning the three girls decided to visit the Pruden Company. It was not listed in the telephone book. Louise called information and asked for the number. She was told that James Pruden, Incorporated, was temporarily disconnected.

"That's strange," she remarked, as she put down the phone.

"Let's see if the police know the firm," Jean suggested.

Louise dialled again, and she was informed that the New York company was a branch of a Canadian firm of fine reputation, which imported china and porcelain.

"But why don't they have a phone?" Louise inquired.

"I really don't know," the officer replied. "Maybe the line is being repaired." He gave the girls the address, and the young detectives set off in a taxi.

They arrived at an office building, went inside, and looked up the company's name on the notice-board. Then they took the lift to the tenth floor. It opened into a large showroom. On display were beautiful dishes and other pieces of china and porcelain.

A receptionist asked if she could help them.

"Is Mr. Pruden in?" Jean inquired.

"Yes," the young woman replied. "Mr. Jim Pruden, Jr. is here. His father is in charge of the Canadian office. What are your names?"

The girls told her, then waited a few minutes before being ushered into a panelled office. A young man with a friendly grin stood up behind his desk and asked them to be seated.

"What can I do for you?" he added.

Louise said, "I understand you import china and porcelain. Do you ever ship that merchandise in kegs?"

Jim Pruden frowned. "What kind of kegs?"

The girl described what the barrels looked like

and explained that they were used for shipping sacramental wine.

Jim Pruden laughed. "You know, that's the funniest thing I've ever heard. I don't think our china would do very well packed in wine."

Louise blushed. "I wasn't implying that the articles were shipped in wine, just in that kind of wooden keg."

Mr. Pruden was still puzzled. "Whatever gives you that idea?"

"Our uncle is captain of the ship *Balaska*," Jean spoke up. "It is in dock right now. My sister saw some crew members rolling kegs to the pier with your name on them."

"What!" the man exclaimed. "It must have been some other Pruden. We have nothing to do with kegs!"

"But it did say James Pruden, Incorporated, New York City," Louise pointed out.

"Was there anything else on the kegs?" Pruden inquired.

Louise told him about the painting of a storm petrel.

The man was completely bewildered by the girls' story. He looked at Louise steadfastly. "You're not pulling my leg, are you?"

"Of course not!"

Pruden went on, "Why are you so interested in those kegs?"

"Our uncle is suspicious that some of his crew may be involved in smuggling activities," Louise explained. "I watched two men unload the kegs off the ship's stern late last evening."

Jim Pruden said he would like to see one of the kegs. "Perhaps they are still on the dock," he declared. "May I come with you?"

"Certainly," Louise said. "But I doubt that you'll find any. They were loaded into a car and taken away."

When the group arrived at the pier, it turned out that she had been right. There was not a single keg to be seen.

"Well, I'd like to speak to the captain, anyway," Jim Pruden said. "I sailed on the *Balaska* a long time ago, but I don't remember the skipper's name. Perhaps he was your uncle."

The girls took Mr. Pruden to Captain Dana's quarters. When they introduced him, Uncle Ned grinned. "You look familiar," he said.

"So do you," the young man replied. "I sat at your table a long time ago when I travelled with my father."

The two men spoke about the voyage for a few minutes, and the girls were glad that Jim Pruden knew Uncle Ned. Now he would no longer be suspicious that they were playing a joke on him.

Then the conversation turned to the kegs.

"I checked the manifest this morning," Captain

Dana said. "There was no merchandise listed for James Pruden, Incorporated. This proves beyond a doubt that someone is using your company's name for underhanded business."

"I'm glad your nieces found out about it," Jim Pruden commented. "My firm could be in a lot of trouble because of those crooked shippers. I'll do my best to find out what's going on."

"So will I," Uncle Ned promised.

After Pruden had left, Captain Dana asked the girls what they were planning to do next. "You really seem to be making good headway on your mystery."

"But this was a false lead," Louise said with a sigh.

"Next I think we should go to Uptown Gems to inquire about Roy Stryker," Jean suggested.

The girls stood up. "We'll either come back here or phone you and let you know what happened, Uncle Ned," Louise added.

The three friends arrived at the jewellery company a half hour later and were introduced to the friendly manager, whose name was Mr. Jacobs. With a disarming smile, Jean inquired, "Does a Roy Stryker work for you?"

"Yes, he's one of our salesmen. Why?"

Jean explained that their uncle was captain of the ship *Balaska*, on which Roy Stryker had been a passenger.

The manager smiled. "He made your acquaintance?"

Louise sidestepped the question. "We were a little curious about his position with you," she said.

"I see," Mr. Jacobs said. "As I told you, he's one of our best salesmen. He just returned from a holiday in Europe."

"Then his trip on the *Balaska* was not on business?" Doris inquired.

"No. Why?"

Jean said bluntly, "Did you know he tried to smuggle something into the country?"

Mr. Jacobs looked shocked. "Are you sure of this?"

The girls nodded. "We were told by a security guard that Stryker tried to bribe him. He wanted to go through customs without having to open his bag."

The manager said he knew nothing about it. "Stryker was on his own. Probably he tried to get some stuff for himself into the United States without paying duty. Obviously it was not enough to get him into trouble. He must have paid whatever he owed. He never mentioned the incident to me or anyone else in the office."

The Danas did not comment, and Jacobs went on, "I've never had any trouble with Stryker. What he does on his own is none of my business, but I'll talk to him nevertheless. We prefer our men to be honest."

The girls thanked the manager, then returned to the ship to tell Captain Dana what they had learned.

"That still doesn't eliminate Stryker as a suspect," the captain said. "Also, Humpmeyer and Bowsky have not come back. I can't believe they jumped ship!"

Just then the telephone rang. Captain Dana picked up the receiver. The girls stood close enough to hear the agitated voice on the other end.

"This is Fred Bowsky speaking," a man said. "I've been kidnapped for spying. I don't know where I am, but Hal Humpmeyer locked me up. He and Yansky—"

There was a click and the line went dead.

"Bowsky?" Uncle Ned called, "Bowsky, are you there?" He jiggled the phone a few times, but it was no use.

"So Humpmeyer and Yansky kidnapped Bowsky!" Jean exclaimed. "I wonder if he had been spying on their activities. Maybe he discovered the secret of the kegs!"

"Maybe, unless this phone call was a hoax," Louise added.

Captain Dana suggested that the girls phone Mrs. Harrington in Oak Falls to see if Yansky had shown up at his apartment.

Jean made the call. To her amazement Mrs. Harrington told her that there had been another break-in at her house the day before. "They took all the petrels," the woman said sadly. "The police found no clues, but they strongly suspect Yansky."

"But Yansky was in New York last night," Jean blurted out. "We were told he was in a discotheque. When we tried to talk to him, he ran away!"

Mrs. Harrington was confused. "How could he have been in New York and Oak Falls at the same time? I don't understand it," she confessed.

Jean had an answer. "Perhaps your thief was Mercek!"

CHAPTER XVI

The *Hi Seas*

When Captain Dana heard the latest news, he frowned. "This case is becoming so complicated, I've lost track of who's who."

"You're not the only one," Jean said. "Let's go over it again and see if we can sort out all suspects. We know that Yansky and Humpmeyer are friends. But did they really kidnap Bowsky, or is he in league with them, too?"

Louise spoke up. "If he were, I doubt he would have mentioned their names when he called."

"Maybe he wanted to get Yansky and Humpmeyer in trouble for some reason," Doris suggested.

Uncle Ned held up one hand. "Let's start with who's accused of what."

"Okay," Jean said. "First, there's Yansky the

witch. He's the one who left the warning about our bad luck and claimed to be the keeper of the storm petrel. Mrs. Harrington's birds were found in his apartment. He either stole them or had them stolen."

Louise took up the story. "Then there's Mercek the thief. He took the chicken petrel from Mrs. Harrington's house. We think either he or Yansky set the fire in our hall closet when Mercek came dressed as a scarecrow to our Halloween party. He also threw Jean overboard."

"And there's Bowsky," Doris said, "who supposedly was kidnapped because he knew too much."

Uncle Ned turned down three fingers. "Who's next?"

"Hal Humpmeyer," Doris said. "He disappeared, and we think he's a smuggler. He's also a friend of Yansky's."

"Then there's Tredway, the dock superintendent of the shipping company," Uncle Ned added. "He may be a smuggler, too. At any rate, he's mixed up with the gang. Is there anyone else?"

"Maybe Stryker, who tried to smuggle something into the country," Louise said.

"And the waiter," Doris said. "He might be in with the petrel gang because he was urging us to leave the ship when the kegs were supposed to be unloaded."

"Seven men," Uncle Ned declared. "Quite a number of suspects."

"There must be other gang members whose names we don't know," Louise said. "For instance, the man who helped Humpmeyer unload the barrels."

"I'd like to do some more sleuthing around the dock," Jean said. "Perhaps we can find more clues by questioning people."

The three girls left at once to start their investigation. The pier was teeming with longshoremen unloading incoming trucks and putting their cargo on the conveyor belt that transported it up into the hold of the *Balaska.*

One of the men, who seemed to be the supervisor, was not actually working. The girls walked up to him, and Louise asked, "Pardon me, but did you see any kegs among the cargo?"

"You mean small barrels like they use for sacramental wine?" he said.

"Yes."

"I haven't seen any around here, but last night when we were loading another ship, I noticed a motorboat with two men in it. They carried a small keg."

"Do you remember the name on the motorboat?"

"It was the *Hi Seas,*" the man replied.

The girls were delighted with this information.

Jean thanked the supervisor, then she and her companions hurried back to Uncle Ned.

Louise asked him if the *Hi Seas* was listed in his maritime directory.

"I'll see," he said and brought the heavy volume from a shelf. He turned to the H's. "No *Hi Seas* in here," he declared. "But I'll call the Coast Guard and see if they've a record of it."

After talking for several minutes to an official, he said, "The *Hi Seas* has recently been registered in New York at an address up the river. Here it is. I wrote it down."

"Let's go there," Jean urged.

Uncle Ned smiled. "I don't blame you for wanting to follow up such a good lead. But I'd rather you wouldn't go alone. I'll get in touch with a police launch and ask the skipper to take you there."

Louise, Jean, and Doris were delighted. In twenty minutes the launch arrived. Uncle Ned accompanied them to the dock and met the skipper, Captain Ramsey, and another policeman. He introduced the girls and added, "My nieces are amateur detectives and have a clue in a smuggling case. They want to check out a lead at this address."

Uncle Ned gave the skipper the piece of paper on which he had written it, then the girls climbed into the small launch. They waved good-bye to Uncle Ned, then the craft chugged off.

"This is exciting!" Louise said as the boat picked up speed. Doris's eyes sparkled. "I'll take a ride like this any day!"

Jean went to talk to the skipper. She told him about the kegs and her suspicion that they might hold something else besides sacramental wine.

Captain Ramsey was impressed. Nevertheless, he said, "Your uncle mentioned that you're amateur detectives. I must say, you look more like school girls to me."

Jean laughed. "We are. But at present we're on holiday because of school repairs."

In a little while the launch turned toward shore and pulled up next to a boathouse. A small cabin cruiser was tied up across its narrow pier.

"I believe this is the place you want," Captain Ramsey announced. "Let's see if we can find the *Hi Seas*."

Louise jumped out of the launch and went up to the motorboat. "It is the *Hi Seas!*" she called out.

Captain Ramsey and the other two girls joined her, and they were about to start for the boathouse when a man appeared around the corner. He seemed surprised to see the police officer.

"Are you looking for someone?" he asked.

Captain Ramsey said, "Yes, we are. Who owns this motorboat?"

"I do."

"Were you out in it last night with another fellow, and did you pick up a keg that was floating near the ocean liner *Balaska?*"

The man looked surprised. "I don't know how you found out, but the answer is yes."

"Had you expected to pick up the keg?" Captain Ramsey went on.

"No. It landed not far from us as we were going by. We didn't even know where it came from, so we took it along."

"Did you open it?" Louise asked.

"Yes, we did. It contained sacramental wine. It was terrible, so I drained it off."

Jean spoke up. "We'd like to have the keg back. Would you let us take it?"

"Sure," the man said.

He disappeared into the boathouse and returned a few minutes later carrying the keg on his right shoulder. He handed it to Captain Ramsey.

"If it isn't a police secret, may I ask why you want this?" he inquired.

The girls did not reply, but the skipper said, "It may or may not have to do with an investigation we're conducting. Thank you very much."

"You're welcome." The man looked after the group with a puzzled expression on his face as they returned to the launch. Captain Ramsey set the keg on the deck. He noticed the name on the label, James Pruden, Incorporated, New York.

"Have you inquired if this belongs to the Pruden Company?" he asked.

Louise nodded. "We went to see Mr. Pruden. He knows nothing about it. That's part of the mystery—who is using his name, and why."

Jean said, "Let's take the keg apart. I want to see if anything's inside."

"All right," Captain Ramsey agreed. He called to the other officer to bring some tools, then asked him to take the wheel. "I'll help the girls with the keg," he added with a grin. "Now let's see how we can tackle this."

He handed Jean a screwdriver. "It was your idea, so you should be the one to try first."

Jean laughed. "Okay," she said, and she took off one of the copper bands that circled the keg. Then she pried away the second one. She half expected the keg to fall apart, but nothing happened.

Captain Ramsey and the other two girls watched her with great interest, wondering what she would do next. Jean tried lifting out the top, then the bottom, but could not budge either part.

"I have a hunch that this keg has two layers, perhaps with a space in between," she said.

"You mean where something valuable could be hidden?" the captain asked.

"Yes." Jean handed the screwdriver to her sister. "Louise, you take a turn."

Louise grinned. "Now that you're having trouble, I'm supposed to help out?"

"That's what sisters are for," Jean laughed.

Louise pried and pried, but made no progress. She was just about to ask the men for help, when Jean spoke up.

"I have an idea. Do you think the storm petrel painted on the side may contain a clue?"

CHAPTER XVII

Deliberate Accident

CAPTAIN Ramsey looked at Jean in astonishment. While she was holding the keg, Louise used the tools deftly, prying around the bird. But nothing happened!

Suddenly Jean said, "I'll bet if there's anything hidden in the bird, it's in the eyes!"

She took a small chisel and hammer, and worked on the petrel's left eye. It would not budge. She tried the right eye and soon realized that it was inlaid with a separate piece of wood. She gouged it out, then exclaimed excitedly, "There's a plug under it!"

While the others watched in fascination, she managed to work the plug loose. Then she stared into the black opening.

"Something shiny's in there!" she said.

"Can you fish it out?" Louise asked eagerly.

"Maybe with a very thin, long pin." The girls examined the array of tools that had been brought to them, but each piece was too large.

"Have you something very small that we could use?" Jean asked Captain Ramsey.

He looked through his pockets, but he found nothing that would fit the little hole. All the while the group had been so intent on trying to discover the secret of the keg that they had failed to notice a powerful motorboat that was approaching them from behind.

When Captain Ramsey stood up to search for another tool, he suddenly saw it only a few feet away from the launch's stern. He shouted to the man at the wheel of the powerboat, who made no attempt to slow or swerve. He was going to ram the launch deliberately!

The girls were terrified. A thought flashed through their minds, "Would it be better to jump into the water?" But there was no time even for this. The next instant there was a splintering crash as the prow of the powerboat hit the launch.

The Danas, Doris, and Captain Ramsey were knocked over, while the pilot held on tightly to the wheel. As Louise went down, she caught a fleeting glimpse of the keg. The impact had lifted it high into the air. The little barrel turned a few times, then splashed into the water!

The powerboat backed away. One of the three

men in it jumped into the waves, grabbed the keg, and tossed it into his boat. Then he swam a few strokes and was pulled in by one of his colleagues. The skipper completed a quick turn and moved away.

Captain Ramsey had hit his head hard on the deck, and it took him a few minutes to clear his brain. When he stood up, he realized what was happening. Angrily he shouted to the men in the powerboat, but they were too far away already and paid no attention.

The girls, meanwhile, had shakily pulled themselves to their feet. They spotted the powerboat as it turned.

"Look!" Louise called out. "The name and number have been covered up!"

The pilot of the small police launch, whose shoulder was hurting from the accident, desperately tried to turn the wheel so they might chase their attacker. There was no response.

"What's the matter?" Captain Ramsey asked.

"The crash has disabled us!" the pilot replied.

Suddenly the others realized that their engine had stopped. Try as he might, the pilot could not start it again. They were stranded in the river!

Captain Ramsey picked up his ship-to-shore telephone. "I'm glad this is still working," he muttered, then he reported the accident and asked for another launch to come and tow them in.

"Would you also send someone after the boat that hit us? It was gray, with its name covered up, and it was quite a bit larger and more powerful than our launch. In the boat are three men who stole a small keg that held sacramental wine. We must recover it!" The captain gave the location where the accident had happened and added, "The fugitives went up the river!"

He was assured that help would be on the way soon. Another launch would try to find the power-boat.

Doris and the Danas felt frustrated. They were bruised, and Doris complained that her arm hurt.

"I'll ask a doctor to examine you as soon as we get to headquarters," Captain Ramsey said, worrying about her already swelling arm.

Louise asked if he had one or two large handkerchiefs. He pulled out one, and the pilot produced another. Louise put them together, then held the four corners and dipped the handkerchiefs into the cold salt water.

"Roll up your sleeve," she said to Doris, then wound the cloth around the girl's arm where it hurt the most. As soon as the compress had warmed, Louise repeated the operation.

"Oh, that feels good," Doris said. "Thanks a lot."

The group began to discuss the accident.

"One thing I'm sure of," Louise said, "is that

the men in the boat were part of the petrel gang." She explained about their enemies and asked Captain Ramsey, "Did you ever hear of them?"

The skipper shook his head. "You say they're smugglers?"

"We think so," Louise replied.

Jean looked off into space and heaved a deep sigh. "The witch's omen!" she said finally.

"What do you mean?" the captain wanted to know, and the girls told him about the unfortunate happenings at their Halloween party.

The skipper frowned. "This sounds like old-time witchcraft. I hope you don't believe any of it."

"We don't believe in omens," Louise replied. "But we suspect the witch is behind all this harassment."

Another police launch arrived. The men in it attached a stout rope to the disabled craft and towed it to a dock where repairs could be made. Captain Ramsey asked if there was any news on the gray powerboat.

"None," an officer replied. "They got away too fast."

The Danas not only felt bad about the incident, but were angry. If the shiny object in the petrel's eye was a diamond, the gang had it back!

Doris's arm was bothering her very much, so Captain Ramsey drove her and the Danas to the nearest hospital for X-rays. Louise and Jean were also examined. It was found that they had only a few cuts and bruises. The X-rays revealed that Doris had not broken her arm, but had sprained it badly. Louise was given credit for her first-aid treatment of cold salt-water compresses, which had kept the arm from swelling even more.

On the way back from the hospital, Captain Ramsey said, "You'd better give up any further sleuthing for the moment. I suggest you go home and take it easy for a while."

The girls agreed, and he dropped them off at the Harlands' apartment. Doris's mother was shocked when she heard what had happened.

"I certainly hope the police will be able to find those wicked men in the powerboat!" she said angrily.

Louise and Jean felt they should call their uncle at once and tell him what they had learned. He, too, was shocked, and more determined than ever to help solve the mystery.

"I'll see you tomorrow," he said. "Today I want you to rest."

A few minutes later, a package was delivered to the Harland home. It was the size of a shoe box and was addressed to Louise and Jean Dana.

"I wonder who sent this," Louise said. "Very few people know we're here."

"Perhaps it's from your aunt," Doris suggested.

"I doubt that. It was hand delivered and has no sender's name on it."

Mrs. Harland examined the package suspiciously. "It doesn't look as if it's from a store, either," she commented.

"We didn't order anything," Louise added.

"Do you think we should open it?" Doris put her hand on the box gingerly.

Mrs. Harland held her back. "It's safer if we take it to police headquarters," she declared. "Too many things have happened lately, and I'm afraid we might all be harmed if we're not careful."

The girls agreed, and she looked at her daughter. "Doris, since your arm still hurts, why don't you stay here and lie down for a while?"

Doris shook her head emphatically. "I wouldn't miss this for the world, Mother. And my arm is fine, really."

Mrs. Harland drove the girls to the nearest police station. They explained why they were afraid to open the package, and an officer, who introduced himself as Captain Craig, took it away.

"I'll have our bomb squad take care of this," he said. "You wait here. It won't take long."

Nervously, the Harlands and the Danas sat down. "I'm sure one of the petrel gang sent us that package," Louise said.

"I wish they'd leave you girls alone!" Mrs. Harland declared. "You've never done anything to any of them. Why do they keep on scaring you?"

"They're afraid we'll find out what they're doing," Jean said.

Soon the officer returned. There was a broad grin on his face as he set the package on the table. "I'm afraid it was a false alarm," he said.

"What's in the box?" Jean urged.

"This," he said and took off the lid.

Everyone stared in surprise. Inside the box lay a dead storm petrel!

CHAPTER XVIII

Telltale Phone Numbers

CAPTAIN Craig lifted the bird from the box. Under the petrel was a note. Jean took it and read it aloud.

"The witch's warning is about to come true."

Louise and Jean sighed. Did this mean more trouble for them?

Captain Craig looked at them curiously. "What kind of difficulties are you in?" he inquired. "This incident is rather strange, to say the least." He pointed to the dead bird and shook his head.

"It is," Louise agreed, and told him about Yansky and his threats, the keg, and the painted petrel on it. "We were just about to uncover something shiny that we felt was smuggled into the United States, when our launch was rammed and the keg stolen."

"Where did this happen?" the captain asked.

"In the Hudson River." Jean took up the story and described the gray powerboat. "The harbour police were unable to catch the people who ran into us," she concluded.

"Possibly they went out to sea," Captain Craig suggested.

"No, they disappeared up the river," Louise said. "If only we could make a search ourselves. Captain Ramsey told us to take it easy for the rest of the day, but we're not in the least bit tired."

Captain Craig's curiosity was thoroughly aroused, and he was impressed by the girls' spunk. "Tell you what," he said. "Perhaps I can arrange for you to go out in a police speedboat to hunt for the craft that followed you. Do you remember the name of it?"

"It's name and number were covered," Jean replied. "But we'd recognize it, anyway. Who'll pilot us?"

"I'll get one of my colleagues from the harbour police to handle the boat," Captain Craig said. He added that he himself was about to go off duty, but would like to accompany the girls.

Mrs. Harland decided to return to the apartment and insisted that Doris accompany her because of her injured arm.

"I hope your search will be successful," she said to the Danas. "And please, be careful!"

"We will," Louise promised. "Besides, we have a fine escort."

Twenty minutes later Captain Craig and the girls climbed into a small speedboat at a nearby police dock. They met their skipper, a lanky young officer named Bruce, and minutes later the group cruised up the eastern bank of the river.

"The boat that rammed you might be docked somewhere," Captain Craig said. "Watch closely for anything that resembles it."

They went far beyond the city limits. However, their search proved in vain.

"I'm afraid we'll have to turn back," Bruce said. "I can only keep the boat out for a couple of hours, then I have to bring it back. Let's go down on the other side. Perhaps we will have better luck there."

He crossed the river, and the group looked in public and private docks on the west bank.

They came to a small marina that bore the sign *Boats for Hire*. Jean spotted a gray craft just like the one that had crashed into them.

"Maybe those men rented the boat," she suggested. "Let's go in and find out."

Captain Craig asked Bruce to pull alongside the dock, then the group jumped out and went into the office. The young man in charge looked amazed at seeing a police officer.

"Can I help you?" he asked quickly.

The captain nodded for Jean to answer. She told what had happened earlier that day to Captain Ramsey's launch and that their attackers had not been found.

"You have a boat outside that looks exactly like the one that rammed us," she added. "By any chance, did you rent it to three men this morning?"

"Yes, we did," the young man replied. "When they brought it back, though, the one who paid me said nothing about an accident, and I didn't notice any damage."

"They could have fixed it before returning the boat," Captain Craig said. "When did they come in?"

"Only a little while ago."

"Were the name and number covered?" Louise inquired.

"No, of course not. Why do you ask?"

"Because something was pasted over them on the craft that rammed us."

"That's strange," the clerk said.

"Do you remember the name of the man who rented the boat?" Captain Craig asked.

"Yes. It was James Johnson. He seemed okay and paid cash for it."

The Danas felt that this was probably not the

man's real name. Jean asked if a small keg had been left on board.

The clerk shook his head. "There was nothing in the craft when it was returned."

"Would you mind if we take a look at the boat ourselves?" the captain suggested.

"No. Go right ahead."

Captain Craig and the girls went outside and boarded the gray powerboat that was moored to the dock. They searched it carefully but saw nothing suspicious. The Danas were about to give up, when Louise's eyes caught a crumpled piece of paper sticking out between two slats in the deck. She picked it up and smoothed the paper as best she could.

"What is it?" Jean asked.

"It seems to be a list of phone numbers," Louise replied. She went down the column of figures with her finger. "Here's Mercek's!" she exclaimed. "His number in Oak Falls!"

"That settles it," Jean declared. "These men are definitely part of the petrel gang!"

Captain Craig looked over her shoulder. His eyes scanned the numbers and suddenly he held out a finger. "Wait a minute. There's one that sounds familiar to me. Let me see if I can remember." He furrowed his brow, but the answer did not come to him.

"I'll call headquarters and ask the desk sergeant to get the information from the phone company," he declared.

The group climbed out of the powerboat and returned to the office. They mentioned nothing to the young man about the paper they had found but requested the use of his telephone. Captain Craig called headquarters and asked to have the familiar number traced.

The officer on the other line recalled it immediately. "That belongs to a sailors' hotel in a rundown area at the waterfront."

After Captain Craig and the girls had left the boat rental office, he passed the information on to them.

"Some of the people involved in your mystery probably live there or at least stay in the place occasionally," he added.

"Let's go and find out!" Jean urged.

Captain Craig agreed to accompany them. "But I don't want you girls to go in until I make an inspection first," he added.

They climbed into the speedboat again and soon arrived at a rickety wharf. Captain Craig and the skipper tied up the craft, then asked the girls to wait while they checked out the hotel.

"It has a pretty bad reputation," the captain explained.

Jean was disappointed. "I wish we could have gone along," she said to Louise. "We might have seen some people we know."

"You mean members of the petrel gang?" Louise asked.

"Yes. Humpmeyer might be there, and perhaps Bowsky, and who knows who else we might meet."

The girls fidgeted and surveyed the waterfront. It was low tide, and dusk was beginning to fall. Jean looked under the wharf. Was she mistaken or did she see a shadow coming their way?

No. She was not wrong. A sailor approached, holding on to the under-wharf beams as he progressed handhold by handhold. Evidently holes had been drilled into the planks to accommodate a man's fingers.

Jean waved to her sister excitedly. "Come and look!" She pointed under the wharf.

Startled, the two watched the man, wondering who he was and why he was moving in this strange fashion.

Finally, the sailor was close enough so that the girls could distinguish his features.

"Hal Humpmeyer!" Jean cried out.

"Yes," the man replied and pulled himself into the speedboat. At the same instant, he emitted a long, low whistle. The girls heard footsteps along the wharf. Were the police returning?

They fervently hoped so, but they were wrong. A gang of toughs raced up to the boat and jumped in.

Two of them grabbed the girls and held hands over their mouths so they could not scream. The captives struggled to get loose, but it was hopeless. Their attackers were too strong.

Humpmeyer glared at them. "Why did you bring the police here?" he demanded.

CHAPTER XIX

The Secret Cellar

THE girls did not answer Humpmeyer's question. They just stared at him, while one of the toughs tried to start the police speedboat. He did not succeed.

"We'd better scram!" he urged.

"But we want our money before we go!" another man spoke up.

Humpmeyer looked at him disdainfully. "You want to be paid for doing nothing?"

"What do you mean? We did what you told us to. We came down here and stopped these girls from leaving."

"But you didn't get the engine running, did you!" Humpmeyer argued. "Now get out!"

The gang glared at him angrily. Suddenly one

of the men punched Humpmeyer on the jaw. The seaman from the *Balaska* punched back. Before Louise and Jean knew what was happening, fists were flying. One of the toughs tried to empty Humpmeyer's pockets and get the money he allegedly owed them. The men who were holding the girls let go of them and yelled, "Hal, give us the pay you promised, or we'll throw you overboard!"

Louise grabbed Jean's hand and whispered, "Now is our chance to escape!"

The men were so busy fighting that they did not notice the Danas climb out of the boat and race down the wharf. Suddenly Humpmeyer realized they were gone. In a panic, he yelled, "You guys let those girls get away! Now they'll report all of us to the cops!"

At this moment Louise saw Captain Craig and their pilot coming toward them. "Hurry!" she shouted.

The officers reached them in a few seconds, and the girls quickly explained what had happened.

"Humpmeyer evidently hired those hoodlums to steal the speedboat and take us away from here!" Jean said.

The policemen did not wait to hear any more and hurried to the boat. One of the gang members glanced up and cried out, "Here comes the law! Scram!"

Two of the toughs disappeared under the wharf while the others jumped into the water. Humpmeyer himself was so dazed from the beating he had received that he seemed unable to move. He stood on deck, staring at the officers with glassy eyes.

"That's Hal Humpmeyer!" Jean cried out as soon as the girls had caught up with the men, and she pointed to the sailor.

Captain Craig and his pilot jumped into the craft and confronted the seaman. Handcuffs were slipped over his wrists before he could resist.

Louise caught sight of the two young gang members who had hidden under the wharf. Apparently they were not aware of the handholds on which Humpmeyer had approached, and they thought there was no way to escape.

She alerted Captain Craig, who ordered the men to come topside. Reluctantly they obeyed. One of them, a gangly fellow with straggly blond hair, said, "We ain't done nothin'!"

"You call jumping into a police boat and scaring these girls nothing?" Captain Craig retorted.

The blond youth looked down at the tips of his shoes.

"We want to ask you some questions," the officer continued. "If you cooperate, we won't arrest you." He nodded toward the girls that they should begin the questioning.

Louise spoke up. "Is Humpmeyer a friend of yours?"

"We never met him before today. He offered to pay us if we would hold you girls until he decided where to take you. He said you double-crossed him. When he went back on his word, we cuffed him around a bit."

"We didn't realize this was a police boat," the other fellow added. "We thought you girls were friends of Humpmeyer's and that this was just a private squabble between you and him."

Captain Craig looked at the young men closely. "I'm warning you. Don't do something like this again, or you'll be in trouble!"

"We won't," the youths promised. "And we didn't mean any harm. Can we go now?"

The captain nodded, and the youths hurried off. Their companions, who had jumped into the water, were pulling themselves up to the wharf some distance away, then ran toward the hotel.

Captain Craig picked up his ship-to-shore radio to report the incident to the harbour police. When he finished speaking, Louise said, "May we contact our uncle, Captain Dana? He'll sign a complaint against Humpmeyer."

The officer handed her the phone. "Good idea. Call him right now."

Hal Humpmeyer glared balefully while Louise told Uncle Ned what had happened.

"I'm glad you found that scoundrel," Captain Dana said. "Where are you taking him? I'll meet you there."

Louise asked Captain Craig for directions to police headquarters, then repeated them to Uncle Ned.

"I'll start out at once," he promised. "By the way, I talked to your Aunt Harriet. She is well and sent a message to you and Jean from Mrs. Harrington."

"What is it?" Louise asked eagerly.

"She mentioned Aesop, who lived many, many years ago and was noted for telling fables. He was also given to pithy sayings. Mrs. Harrington said to tell you this one, 'People often begrudge others what they cannot enjoy themselves.' "

"I wonder why she sent this message," Louise said.

"It certainly fits Humpmeyer," Captain Dana remarked. "Well, I'll see you soon."

The speedboat carried the girls, their prisoner, and the two officers back to the dock where they had obtained the craft. They said good-bye to their pilot, then they drove to headquarters. Uncle Ned had already arrived.

Humpmeyer was advised of his rights and was questioned by the Danas and the police. He was apologetic to Uncle Ned for having taken leave from the *Balaska*, but he would not confess that he had had anything to do with the kegs or the petrel gang. When asked why he wanted to get the girls away from the wharf, he remained tight-lipped. Finally, he was taken to a cell. The Danas thanked Captain Craig for his help, then left headquarters.

"Are you coming to the *Balaska?*" Uncle Ned wanted to know.

"I'd like to go back to that hotel," Jean said. "Would you accompany us? Perhaps we can find out more about Humpmeyer and his cronies."

"Why not?" Uncle Ned said with a smile. "But I'm warning you, it's not a very nice place."

"Captain Craig told us that, too," Louise said. "He wouldn't even let us go inside. But with you I am sure we will have nothing to worry about."

They reached the ramshackle building and walked through the door. The carpet in the lobby was torn and faded. Leather lounge chairs stood along one wall. They were cracked and had open seams in places. A dim bulb lit the shabby interior, and the few men sitting around were seedy-looking.

They eyed Captain Dana and the girls suspiciously and a few made unsavoury remarks. But there was no attempt to stop the callers as they went to the desk. The captain's stately bearing commanded respect.

He addressed the receptionist. "I'd like to see Fred Bowsky."

"Yes sir," the receptionist replied nervously. "Just a minute, sir." He turned to a rack behind him and took off a key. "Bowsky's in Room 210. His roommate had to lock him in because he went berserk."

"I'm sorry to hear that," Uncle Ned replied, taking the key.

He motioned for the girls to follow him. When they were out of earshot of the receptionist, he whispered, "I don't believe that. Something strange is going on here."

There was no lift in the hotel, so the three walked up the stairs and along a hallway until they reached Room 210. After listening for a few moments, Uncle Ned carefully inserted the key. He asked the girls to stand back. Then he opened the door wide.

A haggard-looking man was seated in a chair. A chain was attached to his ankle, with the other end fastened to one leg of the bed. No one else was in the room, which evidently had not been cleaned in weeks.

"Fred Bowsky!" Captain Dana exclaimed.

"Captain Dana! I'm so glad you found me!" the seaman said, a smile flitting across his tired-looking face.

"My nieces are responsible for my being here,"

Uncle Ned replied. "We'll tell you all about it, but first, let me get rid of this chain."

"The key to it is over there on the bureau, out of my reach," Bowsky said.

Quickly the prisoner was released. "We were told by the receptionist that your roommate had to lock you in because you went berserk," Captain Dana said.

"That's a lie!" Bowsky exclaimed. "I have not been ill. But I found out that Hal Humpmeyer and a few of the other seamen are smuggling something into the USA on the *Balaska*. I don't know what, but I wanted to find out, so I asked you for shore leave. I spied on him, but he caught me and brought me here."

"That's wicked!" Louise exclaimed.

"Yes it is," Captain Dana agreed. "How did you manage to phone and tell me about your being kidnapped?"

"Before they chained me to the bed they left the room for a minute, locking me in. I grabbed the phone, but could not talk long because they soon came back."

"Who are they?"

"Hal and his friend Emil Yansky."

"So Yansky's still in New York!" Jean exclaimed.

"I suppose so," Bowsky replied. "I haven't seen him since they chained me up."

"Did you learn anything else about the gang's operation?" Captain Dana inquired.

"Humpmeyer sneaked kegs on the ship in Europe and planned to unload them when most of the crew were gone that night after we docked. He was furious, by the way, when one of the kegs fell overboard because of your niece."

"Do you know what was in the kegs?" Jean asked.

"No. But I heard Hal say that he kept one for himself. He hid it in the cellar of this hotel."

"Do you think it's still there?"

Fred Bowsky shrugged. "I have no idea."

"Let's go down and see!" Jean urged.

Captain Dana looked at the exhausted man in the chair. "Do you feel well enough to come with us?"

"Oh, sure," Bowsky said. "I want to get out of this room as fast as I can."

The group went downstairs and asked the receptionist where the entrance to the cellar was. A look of fright came over the man's face. He pointed to Bowsky. "Does this mean he's all right? He's not crazy?"

Captain Dana assured him that Bowsky was in complete control of all his faculties. "Now show us the way to your basement."

The man left the desk and led them to the kitchen. He pointed to a door, then hurried back while the others turned on the light and went down a rickety stairway.

The large cellar was divided into storage area and furnace and laundry facilities. Another dim light illuminated the part where crates and old furniture was stacked up high. The group began to search there, and a few minutes later they found the keg, which had been hidden behind a pile of boxes. Uncle Ned carried it to the light. Louise and Jean quickly examined it. The petrel painted on it still had both eyes intact.

"Please, Uncle Ned, let's see what's underneath!" Louise requested.

Captain Dana took a penknife from his pocket and opened it. Deftly he circled the right eye with it, then went deeper. Finally he was able to pry out the entire eye and remove the plug underneath it.

The girls stared into the hole. "See, something shiny's in there!" Jean cried out gleefully.

The captain looked for another small tool, which was part of his penknife. Just then Louise said, "I smell gas!"

"I do, too!" Bowsky agreed. "We'd better get out of here."

"Yes," Captain Dana said. "Fred, pick up that keg. We'll take it along."

The seaman grasped the valuable little barrel, and they hurried toward the stairway. They did not get far, however. The gas smell became stronger, and one by one the two men and the girls stumbled, then fell. Within seconds, all of them blacked out!

CHAPTER XX

The Discovery

WHEN Captain Dana, Fred Bowsky, and the girls awoke, they found themselves lying in the hotel's yard. Members of the local rescue squad and the fire department were using respirators to pump oxygen into the victims' lungs. All of them felt shaky and had severe headaches, but were thankful to be alive!

Uncle Ned sat up groggily. "How did we get out here?"

A fireman answered. "The hotel receptionist smelled gas and called us. We put masks on and went into the cellar. It's a good thing we found you when we did."

Louise glanced at the man, who was looking at the group worriedly. "I got suspicious," he said, "and thought I'd better do something."

"Suspicious of what?" she asked him.

The man hesitated. Finally he said, "Humpmeyer's pal, Emil Yansky, arrived at the hotel. When he found out that Bowsky wasn't in Room 210 any longer, he was furious. He asked who let him out. I told him Bowsky was in the basement with a group of people. A sneaky look came over his face. He went to the cellar door, and pretty soon I smelled gas. He must have turned it on."

"Did you see Yansky leave?" Captain Dana asked.

The clerk shook his head. "No, he didn't come back into the lobby. But he could have gone out of the back door."

At this moment a police car roared into the yard. Captain Ramsey jumped out and hurried up to the group. "I understand you were having trouble here," he said. "What happened?"

When he heard the story, the officer looked at Jean and Louise in amazement. "You girls never give up, do you?" he asked. "This time you almost got yourselves killed!"

Louise grinned. "But we found Humpmeyer," she said. "And we know he's in league with Yansky, who tried to suffocate us."

Captain Ramsey nodded. "I have to hand it to you. You've cracked this case wide open. But will you take my advice now and go home to rest? We'll take over for you, I promise."

Captain Dana agreed with the officer and told the girls he would take them back to the Harlands' apartment.

"Could we arrange a meeting at the *Balaska* tomorrow morning?" he requested. "Captain Ramsey, perhaps you and your men will have rounded up some of the gang by then, and we can compare notes."

"Good idea," the officer agreed. "Will you give us a list of all suspects?"

"Well," Louise said, "Hal Humpmeyer is already under arrest. He worked with a man named Emil Yansky, and the two of them locked up Fred Bowsky when he spied on their smuggling. Yansky has a friend named Randy Mercek, who lives in Oak Falls. We suspect he's part of the gang, too. Then there's the shipping line's superintendent, Tredway. He told us that our uncle would be brought up on negligence charges and would be responsible for damages and injuries. No doubt he's part of the gang."

"Also there's Roy Stryker of Uptown Gems," Jean added. "We're not sure if he's connected with the gang, but he should be investigated."

Captain Ramsey promised that he would do all he could. Bowsky knew various places the gang frequented, and the hotel clerk had a list of phone numbers that Humpmeyer had called.

"Perhaps Humpmeyer will change his mind and

confess when we confront him with all this information," Captain Ramsey said.

Suddenly Jean remembered the keg. "What happened to the little barrel we were working on in the basement?" she asked.

"What barrel?" the officer asked.

"The one Humpmeyer had hidden there for his own use. We pried away one of the eyes of the petrel pictured on it and saw something shiny beneath it just before we passed out."

The officer and the Danas went into the cellar, followed by Bowsky. The keg was gone!

"Yansky must have taken it when he turned on the gas!" Captain Dana exclaimed. "This is the second time we lost our evidence!"

"We'll find the keg!" Captain Ramsey vowed. "And we'll report to you tomorrow morning."

The following day, after the Harlands had joined the Danas for a hearty breakfast in Uncle Ned's dining room, Captain Ramsey arrived on board the *Balaska* with the keg over his shoulder. It had been found by the clerk, who had searched the cellar again and discovered that it had rolled out of sight. The officer was followed by a group of police who were escorting a number of handcuffed men into Captain Dana's quarters.

"Wow!" Louise cried out. "It looks as if the whole gang has been rounded up!"

She looked at Humpmeyer, Yansky, Mercek,

and Tredway, then surveyed the other prisoners. There was the waiter who had served dinner in Uncle Ned's quarters the night the kegs were unloaded, and the fellow who had caught the barrels on the dock.

Doris pointed to two other men. "These were the people in the *Petrel* the morning Mercek threw Jean overboard," she said. "I can prove it, because I have their photographs!"

The men glowered, while Jean said, "They were also on the gray powerboat that rammed the police launch in the Hudson River after we retrieved the keg from the *Hi Seas!*"

"Right," Louise said. "Now I recognize them, too. And this is the fellow who dived for the keg." She pointed to a man in overalls who made a face at her.

"What about Roy Stryker?" Doris asked. "Did you have a chance to check him out, Captain Ramsey?"

"We did," the officer replied. "He's clean. Tell me, Captain Dana, are any of these men members of your crew?"

Uncle Ned nodded sadly. "Yes, some are. Yansky is a former crewman, and Tredway, of course, is an employee of the shipping line. Wells over there worked here as a waiter, and Cline, Ruttner, and Molina are regular crew."

Captain Dana's face became hard as he turned to the sailors. "You are an example of men with complete lack of loyalty!" he scolded. "You know I trusted you and gave you a pretty free hand, but you repaid me by using my ship for your underhanded smuggling operation. My only consolation is that you have been caught and will receive appropriate punishment."

Louise looked at Captain Ramsey. "How did you manage to round them all up?"

"With the information that Fred Bowsky gave us and a clue the hotel receptionist added, we found their new hideout."

"You didn't discover any other kegs there, did you?" Captain Dana asked.

"No, but we learned that they were sold to a contact in Chicago, who is already under arrest."

"Did you, by any chance, find a mahogany barometer in the place?" Jean spoke up. "We think Mercek or Yansky stole our uncle's when the fire was set in our hall closet."

"As a matter of fact, I remember seeing one," Captain Ramsey replied. "I'll have one of my men pick it up later so you can identify it."

"I have a question," Doris spoke up. "Why did the gang use the name Pruden on the kegs?"

"Humpmeyer had handled Pruden cargo on a previous trip. He knew Pruden was an importer, and he needed a legitimate name to get the kegs on the *Balaska*. I suppose Pruden sounded as good to him as any."

Jean looked at Yansky. "I don't understand why

you and Mercek came to our house, set the fire, and left the threatening note. We knew nothing about the smuggling!"

"That's right!" Yansky said. "If Humpmeyer hadn't told us to get after you girls, we'd still be in business! What a stupid thing to do!"

Captain Dana looked at Humpmeyer. "Why did your men harrass Jean and Louise?"

"I thought they knew about us," the dejected sailor confessed. "You see, a former buddy of mine and I had an argument. He decided to split. Because he was mad at me, he told me he'd tip off your nieces, who were detectives, and that they'd get right on our case. Afterwards I found out he didn't tell them. But by then it was too late."

"Yeah!" Yansky grumbled.

Humpmeyer glared at him. "If you had done a better job, it would have been all right. These snoopy girls never would have come to New York! You and Randy, a fine pair you were. Couldn't even keep a couple of teenage kids in Oak Falls and off our trail like I told you!"

"Don't blame us!" Yansky defended himself. "It was your idea to send the telegram and have Tredway tell the Danas all that stuff about the *Balaska*. That's why they came to New York!"

"Who broke into Mrs. Harrington's house and stole all her birds?" Jean asked. "Yansky was in New York when that happened."

"Randy did it for me." Yansky shrugged. "He knew I liked birds, so he did me a favour. A lot of good it does me now!"

"He also stole the chicken petrel after the ornithological show, didn't he?" Jean said.

"Sure. Someone told him that Mrs. Harrington bought the bird. But then the stupid thing flew off!"

"You got it anyway because a man caught it and sold it to the pet shop," Louise said.

"You mean that was the same one?" Yansky's eyebrows shot up.

"It was. And who let the cats into Mrs. Harrington's house?"

"I did. I thought I could scare her enough so that she wouldn't tell anyone I took her birds."

"And it was you who sent the dead petrel to our house?" Doris wanted to know.

"Who else?" Humpmeyer growled. "The smart bird lover, of course. Too bad he couldn't think of something more effective to scare you off our case."

"What about the two tickets to the ornithological show in Oak Falls?" Jean wondered. "Who sent them to us?"

"Yansky sent them," Randy Mercek volunteered. "He thought if he set me up there with his bird, I might be able to do something to either scare you or harm you."

"That answers all our questions," Captain Dana said. "All except one."

"What's that?" Doris asked.

"What's in the keg?"

"We haven't had a chance to examine it," Captain Ramsey said. "We thought we'd leave it up to you girls."

Louise and Jean asked Uncle Ned for his pocket knife and immediately began to work on the little barrel. While the others watched, Jean deftly removed the petrel's right eye. She pulled out the plug that was underneath and again noticed something shiny in the tiny hole.

"This time I'm prepared," she said with a smile. From a pocket she took a long, old-fashioned button hook that she had borrowed from Mrs. Harland. She stuck it into the hole, wiggled it around, and pulled. Something moved a fraction of an inch, then there was a distinct click inside the keg.

"You must have triggered a secret mechanism!" Louise exclaimed excitedly. "Let's open the keg and see what it is!"

The girls quickly removed the lid. At once they noticed that one side of the keg had a double wall.

"I suspected that all along," Louise said. "Only we didn't see it before because it was fused at the top. This little trigger behind the eye separated the false lining from the real wall of the barrel."

The opening was too narrow for her to reach in, so Jean turned the keg upside down. Out fell jewellery wrapped in pieces of cloth! There was a diamond necklace, rings, even a thin gold chain belt studded with precious stones!

"I can't believe it!" Doris exclaimed in awe.

"I can't, either," Jean said. "What a haul!"

"You girls did a wonderful job uncovering all this loot!" Captain Ramsey praised them. "The New York Police Department is extremely grateful to you!"

The prisoners looked dejected, and when their guards motioned for them to leave, they followed without a word. After rounds of good-byes with the officers, the Danas and the Harlands sat down, all heaving sighs of relief.

"I wonder what Mrs. Harrington would say about all this," Louise said.

Uncle Ned smiled. "I don't know, but I do know what the Bible says. 'A prudent man forseeth the evil.'" He looked at his nieces fondly. "And I say *thanks, Louise and Jean, for ridding my ship of those troublemakers.*"

THE GHOST IN THE GALLERY

Carolyn Keene

Louise and Jean Dana were rehearsing with their classmates for a musical when a scream echoed through the opera house. The girls stood in silence as they stared up to the dark gallery where a ghostly figure seemed to vanish into thin air.

The manager assured them there was nothing to worry about. But when the young girl detectives investigate they realise they have stumbled on a sinister and chilling mystery that will not be solved until they discover who, or what, is the ghost in the gallery.

THE HAUNTED LAGOON

Carolyn Keene

Through the swirling mists shrouding an isolated lagoon, Louise and Jean Dana watch a fully-rigged sailing ship float in mid-air. A moment later it vanishes. . . .

Never before have the Danas encountered so eerie and baffling a mystery. It begins with an invitation to search for pirate gold off the Virginia coast, and is to test the girls' skills to the utmost as they search for a sea captain who has mysteriously disappeared and are threatened by a sinister enemy who will stop at nothing to prevent them from discovering the truth.

Pirates, ghosts and buried treasure all add to the suspense as Louise and Jean follow the twisting trail of clues to a startling climax.

Dana Girls Mystery No. 8: A series from the author of the Nancy Drew Books.

MYSTERY OF THE BAMBOO BIRD

Carolyn Keene

When a bamboo Garuda bird containing a sacred gold statue is stolen from Malee Wongsuwan at Starhurst School, she begs her friends, Louise and Jean Dana, to help in the recovery of her treasured possessions.

Despite the threat of danger, the young detectives agree to take the case — and find themselves involved in one of the most exciting and intriguing adventures they've ever encountered. They pursue the thief across the United States and on to Malee's homeland, Thailand, where a trail of puzzling clues and a series of harrowing experiences await them among the magnificent temples and picturesque canals of Bangkok.

Dana Girl Mystery No. 9: A series from the author of the Nancy Drew Books.

THE SECRET OF LOST LAKE

Carolyn Keene

While searching for a runaway dog in the Rocky Mountains, Louise and Jean Dana learn about the mystery of Lost Lake. Over forty years ago an isolated town was buried in a landslide and now a mysterious old woman seems to guard its secret. When the young girl detectives discover a message scrawled on the wall of an Indian cave they begin to realize there is a sinister plot afoot.

Dana Girls Mystery No. 11: A series from the author of the Nancy Drew Books.

THE SIERRA GOLD MYSTERY

Carolyn Keene

The Dana girls' Aunt Carol has asked them to drop everything and come out to California to help her solve a mystery. Louise and Jean are eager to start a new case — but not even they can imagine what lies in store for them this time. Awaiting them in California is not one mystery but three, each more intriguing than the next, and a surprising string of clues that leads the young detectives to the historic Sierra Nevada mountain range and a treasure that has been buried for over a hundred years.

Dana Girls Mystery No. 10: A series from the author of the Nancy Drew books.

THE WINKING RUBY MYSTERY

Carolyn Keene

'Save Carlo. . . winking ruby. . . hurry!' The plea came from a young violinist only seconds before he lapsed into a coma. But it was enough to launch Louise and Jean Dana on one of the most exciting and most terrible adventures of their lives. From the moment they board the 'Balaska', the teenage detectives sense that they are in danger — but even they cannot imagine just how serious it is to become.

Dana Girls Mystery No. 12: A series from the author of the Nancy Drew Books.

MYSTERY OF THE STONE TIGER

Carolyn Keene

Dana Girls Mystery No. 1: A series from the author of the Nancy Drew Books.

A black-robed ghost stalks the streets of Oak Falls . . .

A tiger roams the woods on the outskirts of town . . .

The Hilary Museum is haunted by a phantom prowler who passes through locked doors and bolted windows. The police are baffled and the whole town is frightened. In desperation, Elise Hilary begs the Dana girls to solve the awful mystery surrounding her museum. Determined to unravel the eerie puzzle, Louise and Jean Dana take on the job and involve themselves in a series of frightening adventures as they follow a twisting maze of clues to find the solution of this exciting mystery.

MYSTERY OF THE WAX QUEEN

Carolyn Keene

Dana Girls Mystery No. 4 : A series from the author of the Nancy Drew books.

The teenage sleuths, Louise and Jean Dana, are thrilled when their uncle asks them to solve an unusual and fascinating mystery. A bust of Queen Victoria suddenly appears in the window of a shop in New York City, and then just as quickly disappears in the strangest of circumstances. As the Danas determinedly follow the puzzling clues – which lead them to a sculptress with amazing psychic powers – there are people equally determined to scare them off the case.

THE SECRET OF THE SILVER DOLPHIN

Carolyn Keene

Dana Girls Mystery no. 3: A series from the author of the Nancy Drew Books.

Judy Platt is desperately trying to find the silver dolphin mentioned in her dead brother's will – but no one knows whether the lost dolphin is a live mammal or a silver ornament. When Louise and Jean Dana hear a newscast announcing a reward to anyone who can locate the dolphin, they immediately take up the challenge to solve the strange mystery.

Their dangerous quest for the mysterious dolphin leads them to a deserted Caribbean island where they find themselves caught up in one of the most exciting and baffling adventures they have ever faced.

THE RIDDLE OF THE FROZEN FOUNTAIN

Carolyn Keene

Dana Girls Mystery No. 2: A series from the author of the Nancy Drew books.

Mysteries have a way of finding the Dana girls, no matter where they are. This time it all begins when Professor Crandall of Starhurst School receives an anonymous note, warning him not to remove the valuable bronze fountain that he has just purchased from an estate nearby. Louise and Jean courageously set out to track down the writer of the threatening note – and in doing so become deeply enmeshed in a series of bizarre and baffling events, including the midnight appearance of phantom ice skaters on the school pond.